NO FEAR
SHAKESPEARE™

NO FEAR
SHAKESPEARE™

The Merchant of Venice

DELUXE STUDENT EDITION

There's matter in these sighs, these
profound heaves. You must translate.
'Tis fit we understand them.

(*Hamlet, 4.1.*)

Have you ever found yourself looking at a Shakespeare
play, then down at the footnotes, then back up at the play,
and still not understanding? You know what the individual
words mean, but they don't add up. SparkNotes' *No Fear
Shakespeare* will help you break through all that. Put the
pieces together with our easy-to-read translations. Soon
you'll be reading Shakespeare's own words fearlessly—
and actually enjoying it.

No Fear Shakespeare puts Shakespeare's language side-by-
side with a facing-page translation into modern English—
the kind of English people actually speak today. When
Shakespeare's words make your head spin, our translation
will help you sort out what's happening, who's saying
what, and why.

*sparknotes

SPARKNOTES and NO FEAR SHAKESPEARE
are registered trademarks of SparkNotes LLC.

Play translation and notes © 2003 Spark Publishing
Expanded study guide material and cover © 2019, 2020 SparkNotes LLC

This 2020 edition printed for SparkNotes LLC by Sterling Publishing Co., Inc.

ISBN 978-1-4114-7968-5

Distributed in Canada by Sterling Publishing Co., Inc.
c/o Canadian Manda Group, 664 Annette Street
Toronto, Ontario M6S 2C8, Canada
Distributed in the United Kingdom by GMC Distribution Services
Castle Place, 166 High Street, Lewes, East Sussex BN7 1XU, England
Distributed in Australia by NewSouth Books
University of New South Wales, Sydney, NSW 2052, Australia

For information about custom editions, special sales, and premium
and corporate purchases, please contact Sterling Special Sales at
800-805-5489 or specialsales@sterlingpublishing.com.

Manufactured in Canada

Lot #:

2 4 6 8 10 9 7 5 3 1

09/20

sterlingpublishing.com
sparknotes.com

Cover design by Elizabeth Mihaltse Lindy
Interior design by Sharon Jacobs

CONTENTS

PART I

LITERATURE GUIDE

PART II

THE PLAY

PART III

STUDY GUIDE

NOTES

PART I

LITERATURE GUIDE

NOTES

1

CONTEXT

THE MOST INFLUENTIAL WRITER in all of English literature, William Shakespeare was born in 1564 to a successful middle-class glover in Stratford-upon-Avon, England. Shakespeare attended grammar school, but his formal education proceeded no further. In 1582 he married an older woman, Anne Hathaway, and had three children with her. Around 1590 he left his family behind and traveled to London to work as an actor and playwright. Public and critical acclaim quickly followed, and Shakespeare eventually became the most popular playwright in England and part-owner of the Globe Theater. His career bridged the reigns of Elizabeth I (ruled 1558–1603) and James I (ruled 1603–1625), and he was a favorite of both monarchs. Indeed, James granted Shakespeare's company the greatest possible compliment by bestowing upon its members the title of King's Men. Wealthy and renowned, Shakespeare retired to Stratford and died in 1616 at the age of fifty-two. At the time of Shakespeare's death, literary luminaries such as Ben Jonson hailed his works as timeless.

Shakespeare's works were collected and printed in various editions in the century following his death, and by the early eighteenth century, his reputation as the greatest poet ever to write in English was well established. The unprecedented admiration garnered by his works led to a fierce curiosity about Shakespeare's life, but the dearth of biographical information has left many details of Shakespeare's personal history shrouded in mystery. Some people have concluded from this fact and from Shakespeare's modest education that Shakespeare's plays were actually written by someone else—Francis Bacon and the Earl of Oxford are the two most popular candidates—but the support for this claim is overwhelmingly circumstantial, and the theory is not taken seriously by many scholars.

In the absence of credible evidence to the contrary, Shakespeare must be viewed as the author of the thirty-seven plays and 154 sonnets that bear his name. The legacy of this body of work is immense. A number of Shakespeare's plays seem to have transcended even the category of brilliance, becoming so influential as to affect profoundly the course of Western literature and culture ever after.

The Merchant of Venice was probably written in either 1596 or 1597, after Shakespeare had written such plays as *Romeo and Juliet* and *Richard III*, but before he penned the great tragedies of his later years. Its basic plot outline, with the characters of the merchant, the poor suitor, the fair lady, and the villainous Jew, is found in a number of contemporary Italian story collections, and Shakespeare borrowed several details, such the choice of caskets that Portia inflicts on all her suitors, from preexisting sources. *The Merchant of Venice*'s Italian setting and marriage plot are typical of Shakespeare's earlier comedies, but the characters of Portia, Shakespeare's first great heroine, and the unforgettable villain Shylock elevate this play to a new level.

Shylock's cries for a pound of flesh have made him one of literature's most memorable villains, but many readers and playgoers have found him a compelling and sympathetic figure. The question of whether or not Shakespeare endorses the anti-Semitism of the Christian characters in the play has been much debated. Jews in Shakespeare's England were a marginalized group, and Shakespeare's contemporaries would have been very familiar with portrayals of Jews as villains and objects of mockery. For example, Christopher Marlowe's *The Jew of Malta*, a bloody farce about a murderous Jewish villain, was a great popular success and would have been fresh in Shakespeare's mind as he set about creating his own Jewish character. Shakespeare certainly draws on this anti-Semitic tradition in portraying Shylock, exploiting Jewish stereotypes for comic effect. But Shylock is a more complex character than the Jew in Marlowe's play, and Shakespeare makes him seem more human by showing that his hatred is born of the mistreatment he has suffered in a Christian society. Shakespeare's character includes an element of pathos as well as comedy, meaning that he elicits from readers and audiences pity and compassion, rather than simply scorn and derision.

2

PLOT OVERVIEW

ANTONIO, A VENETIAN MERCHANT, complains to his friends of a melancholy that he cannot explain. His friend Bassanio is desperately in need of money to court Portia, a wealthy heiress who lives in the nearby city of Belmont. Bassanio asks Antonio for a loan in order to travel in style to Portia's estate. Antonio agrees, but is unable to make the loan himself because his own money is all invested in a number of trade ships that are still at sea. Antonio suggests that Bassanio secure the loan from one of the city's moneylenders and name Antonio as the loan's guarantor. In Belmont, Portia expresses sadness over the terms of her father's will, which stipulates that she must marry the man who correctly chooses one of three caskets. None of Portia's current suitors is to her liking, and she and her lady-in-waiting, Nerissa, fondly remember a visit paid some time before by Bassanio.

In Venice, Antonio and Bassanio approach Shylock, a Jewish moneylender, for a loan. Shylock nurses a long-standing grudge against Antonio, who has made a habit of berating Shylock and other Jews for their practice of loaning money at exorbitant rates of interest, and who undermines their business by offering interest-free loans. Although Antonio refuses to apologize for his behavior, Shylock acts agreeably and offers to lend Bassanio three thousand ducats with no interest. Shylock adds, however, that should the loan go unpaid, Shylock will be entitled to a pound of Antonio's own flesh. Despite Bassanio's warnings, Antonio agrees. In Shylock's own household, his servant Launcelot decides to leave Shylock's service to work for Bassanio, and Shylock's daughter

Jessica schemes to elope with Antonio's friend Lorenzo. That night, the streets of Venice fill up with revelers, and Jessica escapes with Lorenzo by dressing as his page. After a night of celebration, Bassanio and his friend Gratiano leave for Belmont, where Bassanio intends to win Portia's hand.

In Belmont, Portia welcomes the prince of Morocco, who has come in an attempt to choose the right casket to marry her. The prince studies the inscriptions on the three caskets and chooses the gold one, which proves to be an incorrect choice. In Venice, Shylock is furious to find that his daughter has run away, but rejoices in the fact that Antonio's ships are rumored to have been wrecked and that he will soon be able to claim his debt. In Belmont, the prince of Arragon also visits Portia. He, too, studies the caskets carefully, but he picks the silver one, which is also incorrect. Bassanio arrives at Portia's estate, and they declare their love for one another. Despite Portia's request that he wait before choosing, Bassanio immediately picks the correct casket, which is made of lead. He and Portia rejoice, and Gratiano confesses that he has fallen in love with Nerissa. The couples decide on a double wedding. Portia gives Bassanio a ring as a token of love, and makes him swear that under no circumstances will he part with it. They are joined, unexpectedly, by Lorenzo and Jessica. The celebration, however, is cut short by the news that Antonio has indeed lost his ships, and that he has forfeited his bond to Shylock. Bassanio and Gratiano immediately travel to Venice to try and to Antonio's life. After they leave, Portia tells Nerissa that they will go to Venice disguised as men.

Shylock ignores the many pleas to spare Antonio's life, and a trial is called to decide the matter. The duke of Venice, who presides over the trial, announces that he has sent for a legal expert, who turns out to be Portia disguised as a young man of law. Portia asks Shylock to show mercy, but he remains inflexible and insists the pound of flesh is rightfully his. Bassanio offers Shylock twice the money due him, but Shylock insists on collecting the bond as it is written. Portia examines the contract and, finding it legally binding, declares that Shylock is entitled to the merchant's flesh. Shylock ecstatically praises her wisdom; but as he is on the verge of collecting his due, Portia reminds him that he must do so without causing Antonio to bleed, as the contract does not entitle him to any blood. Trapped by this logic, Shylock hastily agrees to take Bassanio's money instead, but Portia insists that Shylock take his bond as written, or nothing at all. Portia informs Shylock that he is guilty of conspiring against the life of a Venetian citizen, which means he must turn over half of his property to the state and the other half to Antonio. The duke spares Shylock's life and takes a fine instead of Shylock's property. Antonio also forgoes his half of Shylock's wealth on two conditions: first, Shylock must convert to Christianity; and second, he must will the entirety of his estate to Lorenzo and Jessica upon his death. Shylock agrees and takes his leave.

Bassanio, who does not see through Portia's disguise, showers the young law clerk with thanks, and is eventually pressured into giving Portia the ring with which he promised never to part. Gratiano gives Nerissa, who is disguised as Portia's clerk, his ring. The two women return to Belmont, where they find Lorenzo and Jessica declaring their love to each other under the moonlight. When Bassanio and Gratiano arrive the next day, their wives accuse them of faithlessly giving their rings to other women. Before the deception goes too far, however, Portia reveals that she was, in fact, the law clerk, and both she and Nerissa reconcile with their husbands. Lorenzo and Jessica are pleased to learn of their inheritance from Shylock, and the joyful news arrives that Antonio's ships have in fact made it back safely. The group celebrates its good fortune.

3

IN-DEPTH REVIEW OF CHARACTERS

SHYLOCK

A Jewish moneylender in Venice. Angered by his mistreatment at the hands of Venice's Christians, particularly Antonio, Shylock schemes to eke out his revenge by ruthlessly demanding as payment a pound of Antonio's flesh. Although seen by the rest of the play's characters as an inhuman monster, Shylock at times diverges from stereotype and reveals himself to be quite human. These contradictions, and his eloquent expressions of hatred, have earned Shylock a place as one of Shakespeare's most memorable characters.

PORTIA

A wealthy heiress from Belmont. Portia's beauty is matched only by her intelligence. Bound by a clause in her father's will that forces her to marry whichever suitor chooses the correct among three caskets, Portia is still able to marry her true love, Bassanio when he selects the casket with her portrait inside. The cleverest character in the play, Portia, disguised as a young law clerk, saves Antonio from Shylock's knife.

ANTONIO

The merchant whose love for his friend Bassanio prompts him to sign Shylock's contract and almost lose his life. Antonio is something of a mercurial figure, often inexplicably melancholy and, as Shylock points out, possessed of an incorrigible dislike of Jews. Nonetheless, Antonio is beloved of his friends and proves merciful to Shylock, albeit with conditions.

BASSANIO

A gentleman of Venice, and a kinsman and dear friend to Antonio. Bassanio's love for the wealthy Portia leads him to borrow money from Shylock with Antonio as his guarantor. An ineffectual businessman, Bassanio proves himself a worthy suitor, correctly identifying the casket that contains Portia's portrait.

GRATIANO

A friend of Bassanio's who accompanies him to Belmont. A coarse and garrulous young man, Gratiano is Shylock's most vocal and insulting critic during the trial. While Bassanio courts Portia, Gratiano falls in love with and eventually weds Portia's lady-in-waiting, Nerissa.

JESSICA

Although she is Shylock's daughter, Jessica hates life in her father's house, and elopes with the young Christian gentleman Lorenzo. The fate of her soul is often in doubt: the play's characters wonder if her marriage can overcome the fact that she was born a Jew, and we wonder if her sale of a ring given to her father by her mother is excessively callous.

LORENZO

A friend of Bassanio and Antonio, Lorenzo is in love with Shylock's daughter, Jessica. He schemes to help Jessica escape from her father's house, and he eventually elopes with her to Belmont.

NERISSA

Portia's lady-in-waiting and confidante. She marries Gratiano and escorts Portia on Portia's trip to Venice by disguising herself as her law clerk.

LAUNCELOT GOBBO

Bassanio's servant. A comical, clownish figure who is especially adept at making puns, Launcelot leaves Shylock's service in order to work for Bassanio.

THE PRINCE OF MOROCCO

A Moorish prince who seeks Portia's hand in marriage. The prince of Morocco asks Portia to ignore his dark countenance and seeks to win her by picking one of the three caskets. Certain that the caskets reflect Portia's beauty and stature, the prince of Morocco picks the gold chest, which proves to be incorrect.

THE PRINCE OF ARRAGON

An arrogant Spanish nobleman who also attempts to win Portia's hand by picking a casket. Like the prince of Morocco, however, the prince of Arragon chooses unwisely. He picks the silver casket, which gives him a message calling him an idiot instead of Portia's hand.

SALARINO

A Venetian gentleman, and friend to Antonio, Bassanio, and Lorenzo. Salarino escorts the newlyweds Jessica and Lorenzo to Belmont, and returns with Bassanio and Gratiano for Antonio's trial. He is often almost indistinguishable from his companion Solanio.

SOLANIO

A Venetian gentleman, and frequent counterpart to Salarino.

THE DUKE OF VENICE

The ruler of Venice, who presides over Antonio's trial. Although a powerful man, the duke's state is built on respect for the law, and he is unable to help Antonio.

OLD GOBBO

Launcelot's father, also a servant in Venice.

TUBAL

A Jew in Venice, and one of Shylock's friends.

DOCTOR BELLARIO

A wealthy Paduan lawyer and Portia's cousin. Doctor Bellario never appears in the play, but he gives Portia's servant the letters of introduction needed for her to make her appearance in court.

BALTHASAR

Portia's servant, whom she dispatches to get the appropriate materials from Doctor Bellario.

CHAPTER

4

ANALYSIS OF MAJOR CHARACTERS

SHYLOCK

Although critics tend to agree that Shylock is *The Merchant of Venice*'s most noteworthy figure, no consensus has been reached on whether to read him as a bloodthirsty bogeyman, a clownish Jewish stereotype, or a tragic figure whose sense of decency has been fractured by the persecution he endures. Certainly, Shylock is the play's antagonist, and he is menacing enough to seriously imperil the happiness of Venice's businessmen and young lovers alike. Shylock is also, however, a creation of circumstance; even in his single-minded pursuit of a pound of flesh, his frequent mentions of the cruelty he has endured at Christian hands make it hard for us to label him a natural-born monster. In one of Shakespeare's most famous monologues, for example, Shylock argues that Jews are humans and calls his quest for vengeance the product of lessons taught to him by the cruelty of Venetian citizens. On the other hand, Shylock's coldly calculated attempt to revenge the wrongs done to him by murdering his persecutor, Antonio, prevents us from viewing him in a primarily positive light. Shakespeare gives us unmistakably human moments, but he often steers us against Shylock as well, painting him as a miserly, cruel, and prosaic figure.

PORTIA

Quick-witted, wealthy, and beautiful, Portia embodies the virtues that are typical of Shakespeare's heroines—it is no surprise that she emerges as the antidote to Shylock's malice. At the beginning of the play, however, we do not see Portia's potential for initiative and resourcefulness, as she is a near prisoner, feeling herself absolutely bound to follow her father's dying wishes. This opening appearance, however, proves to be a revealing introduction to Portia, who emerges as that rarest of combinations—a free spirit who abides rigidly by rules. Rather than ignoring the stipulations of her father's will, she watches a stream of suitors pass her by, happy to see these particular suitors go, but sad that she has no choice in the matter. When Bassanio arrives, however, Portia proves herself to be highly resourceful, begging the man she loves to stay a while before picking a chest, and finding loopholes in the will's provision that we never thought possible. Also, in her defeat of Shylock Portia prevails by applying a more rigid standard than Shylock himself, agreeing that his contract very much entitles him to his pound of flesh, but adding that it does not allow for any loss of blood. Anybody can break the rules, but Portia's effectiveness comes from her ability to make the law work for her.

Portia rejects the stuffiness that rigid adherence to the law might otherwise suggest. In her courtroom appearance, she vigorously applies the law, but still flouts convention by appearing disguised as a man. After depriving Bassanio of his ring, she stops the prank before it goes too far, but still takes it far enough to berate Bassanio and Gratiano for their callousness, and she even insinuates that she has been unfaithful.

ANTONIO

Although the play's title refers to him, Antonio is a rather lackluster character. He emerges in Act 4, scene 1 as a hopeless depressive, someone who cannot name the source of his melancholy and who, throughout the course of the play, devolves into a self-pitying lump, unable to muster the energy required to defend himself against execution. Antonio never names the cause of his melancholy, but the evidence seems to point to his being in love, despite his denial of this idea in Act I, scene i. The most likely object of his affection is Bassanio, who takes full advantage of the merchant's boundless feelings for him. Antonio has risked the entirety of his fortune on overseas trading ventures, yet he agrees to guarantee the potentially lethal loan Bassanio secures from Shylock. In the context of his unrequited and presumably unconsummated relationship with Bassanio, Antonio's willingness to offer up a pound of his own flesh seems particularly important, signifying a union that grotesquely alludes to the rites of marriage, where two partners become "one flesh."

Further evidence of the nature of Antonio's feelings for Bassanio appears later in the play, when Antonio's proclamations resonate with the hyperbole and self-satisfaction of a doomed lover's declaration: "Pray God Bassanio come / To see me pay his debt, and then I care not" (3.3.). Antonio ends the play as happily as he can, restored to wealth even if not delivered into love. Without a mate, he is indeed the "tainted wether"—or castrated ram—of the flock, and he will likely return to his favorite pastime of moping about the streets of Venice (4.1.). After all, he has effectively disabled himself from pursuing his other hobby—abusing Shylock—by insisting that the Jew convert to Christianity. Although a sixteenth-century audience might have seen this demand as merciful, as Shylock is saving himself from eternal damnation by converting, we are less likely to be convinced. Not only does Antonio's reputation as an anti-Semite precede him, but the only instance in the play when he breaks out of his doldrums is his "storm" against Shylock (1.3.). In this context, Antonio proves that the dominant threads of his character are melancholy and cruelty.

PART II

THE PLAY

5

The Merchant of Venice

THE ORIGINAL PLAY
WITH A MODERN TRANSLATION

William Shakespeare

NO FEAR SHAKESPEARE

CHARACTER LIST*

Shylock

Portia

Antonio

Bassanio

Gratiano

Jessica

Lorenzo

Nerissa

Launcelot Gobbo

The Prince of Morocco

The Prince of Arragon

Salarino

Solanio

The Duke of Venice

Old Gobbo

Tubal

Doctor Bellario

Balthazar

*See page 11 for an in-depth review of the characters.

ACT ONE

ACT TWO

ACT THREE

ACT FOUR

ACT FIVE

ACT I

Scene 1

Enter ANTONIO, SALARINO, *and* SOLANIO

ANTONIO
In sooth, I know not why I am so sad.
It wearies me; you say it wearies you.
But how I caught it, found it, or came by it,
What stuff 'tis made of, whereof it is born,
5 I am to learn.
And such a want-wit sadness makes of me,
That I have much ado to know myself.

SALARINO
Your mind is tossing on the ocean,
There, where your argosies with portly sail,
10 Like signors and rich burghers on the flood—
Or, as it were, the pageants of the sea—
Do overpeer the petty traffickers
That curtsy to them, do them reverence
As they fly by them with their woven wings.

SOLANIO
15 Believe me, sir, had I such venture forth,
The better part of my affections would
Be with my hopes abroad. I should be still
Plucking the grass to know where sits the wind,
Peering in maps for ports and piers and roads.
20 And every object that might make me fear
Misfortune to my ventures out of doubt
Would make me sad.

ACT I

Scene 1

ANTONIO, SALARINO, *and* SOLANIO *enter.*

ANTONIO

To be honest, I don't know why I'm so sad. I'm tired of it, and you say you're tired of it too. But I have no idea how I got so depressed. And if I can't figure out what's making me depressed, I must not understand myself very well.

SALARINO

You're worried about your ships. Your mind is out there getting tossed around on the ocean with them. But they're fine. They're like huge parade floats on the sea. They're so big they look down on the smaller ships, which all have to bow and then get out of the way. Your ships fly like birds past those little boats.

SOLANIO

Yes, believe me, if I had such risky business ventures in other countries, I'd be sad too. I'd worry about it every second. I'd constantly be tossing blades of grass into the air to find out which way the wind was blowing. I'd be peering over maps to figure out the best ports, piers, and waterways. Everything that made me worry about my ships would make me sad.

SALARINO
                                        My wind cooling my broth
Would blow me to an ague when I thought
What harm a wind too great at sea might do.
25   I should not see the sandy hourglass run,
But I should think of shallows and of flats
And see my wealthy Andrew docked in sand,
Vailing her high top lower than her ribs
To kiss her burial. Should I go to church
30   And see the holy edifice of stone
And not bethink me straight of dangerous rocks,
Which, touching but my gentle vessel's side,
Would scatter all her spices on the stream,
Enrobe the roaring waters with my silks,
35   And, in a word, but even now worth this,
And now worth nothing? Shall I have the thought
To think on this, and shall I lack the thought
That such a thing bechanced would make me sad?
But tell not me. I know Antonio
40   Is sad to think upon his merchandise.

ANTONIO
Believe me, no. I thank my fortune for it—
My ventures are not in one bottom trusted,
Nor to one place, nor is my whole estate
Upon the fortune of this present year.
45   Therefore my merchandise makes me not sad.

SOLANIO
Why then, you are in love.

ANTONIO
                                        Fie, fie!

SOLANIO
Not in love neither? Then let us say you are sad
Because you are not merry—and 'twere as easy
For you to laugh and leap and say you are merry
50   Because you are not sad. Now, by two-headed Janus,
Nature hath framed strange fellows in her time.

SALARINO

I'd get scared every time I blew on my soup to cool it, thinking of how a strong wind could wipe out my ships. Every time I glanced at the sand in an hourglass I'd imagine my ships wrecked on sandbars. I'd think of dangerous rocks every time I went to church and saw the stones it was made of. If my ship brushed up against rocks like that, its whole cargo of spices would be dumped into the sea. All of its silk shipments would be sent flying into the roaring waters. In one moment I'd go bankrupt. Who wouldn't get sad thinking about things like that? It's obvious. Antonio is sad because he's so worried about his cargo.

ANTONIO

No, that's not it, trust me. Thankfully my financial situation is healthy. I don't have all of my money invested in one ship, or one part of the world. If I don't do well this year, I'll still be okay. So it's not my business that's making me sad.

SOLANIO

Well, then, you must be in love.

ANTONIO

Oh, give me a break.

SOLANIO

You're not in love either? Fine, let's just say you're sad because you're not in a good mood. You know, it'd be just as easy for you to laugh and dance around and say you're in a good mood. You could just say you're not sad. Humans are so different.

Some that will evermore peep through their eyes
And laugh like parrots at a bagpiper,
And other of such vinegar aspect
55   That they'll not show their teeth in way of smile
Though Nestor swear the jest be laughable.

Enter BASSANIO, LORENZO, *and* GRATIANO

Here comes Bassanio, your most noble kinsman,
Gratiano, and Lorenzo. Fare ye well.
We leave you now with better company.

SALARINO
60   I would have stayed till I had made you merry
If worthier friends had not prevented me.

ANTONIO
Your worth is very dear in my regard.
I take it your own business calls on you
And you embrace th' occasion to depart.

SALARINO
(to BASSANIO, LORENZO, GRATIANO*)*
65   Good morrow, my good lords.

BASSANIO
(to SALARINO *and* SOLANIO*)*
Good signors both, when shall we laugh? Say, when?
You grow exceeding strange. Must it be so?

SALARINO
We'll make our leisures to attend on yours.

Exeunt SALARINO *and* SOLANIO

LORENZO
My Lord Bassanio, since you have found Antonio,
70   We two will leave you. But at dinnertime
I pray you have in mind where we must meet.

BASSANIO
I will not fail you.

Some people will laugh at anything, and others are so grouchy they won't even crack a smile when they hear something hysterically funny.

BASSANIO, LORENZO, *and* GRATIANO *enter.*

Here comes your cousin Bassanio. And Gratiano and Lorenzo too. Goodbye, then. We'll leave you to talk to them. They're better company.

SALARINO

I would've stayed to cheer you up, if your nobler friends hadn't shown up.

ANTONIO

You're both very precious to me. But I understand. You need to leave to take care of your own business.

SALARINO

(to BASSANIO, LORENZO, *and* GRATIANO*)* Good morning, gentlemen.

BASSANIO

(to SALARINO *and* SOLANIO*)* Hello, friends. When are we going to have fun together again? Just name the time. We never see you anymore. Does it have to be that way?

SALARINO

Let us know when you want to get together. We're available.

SALARINO *and* SOLANIO *exit.*

LORENZO

Bassanio, we'll say goodbye for now, since you've found Antonio. But don't forget, we're meeting for dinner tonight.

BASSANIO

Don't worry, I'll be there.

ACT ONE

GRATIANO
You look not well, Signor Antonio.
You have too much respect upon the world.
75 They lose it that do buy it with much care.
Believe me, you are marvelously changed.

ANTONIO
I hold the world but as the world, Gratiano—
A stage where every man must play a part,
And mine a sad one.

GRATIANO
                                        Let me play the fool.
80 With mirth and laughter let old wrinkles come.
And let my liver rather heat with wine
Than my heart cool with mortifying groans.
Why should a man whose blood is warm within
Sit like his grandsire cut in alabaster,
85 Sleep when he wakes, and creep into the jaundice
By being peevish? I tell thee what, Antonio—
I love thee, and 'tis my love that speaks—
There are a sort of men whose visages
Do cream and mantle like a standing pond,
90 And do a willful stillness entertain
With purpose to be dressed in an opinion
Of wisdom, gravity, profound conceit,
As who should say, "I am Sir Oracle,
And when I ope my lips, let no dog bark!"
95 O my Antonio, I do know of these
That therefore only are reputed wise
For saying nothing, when I am very sure
If they should speak, would almost damn those ears
Which, hearing them, would call their brothers fools.
100 I'll tell thee more of this another time.
But fish not with this melancholy bait
For this fool gudgeon, this opinion.—
Come, good Lorenzo.—Fare ye well awhile.
I'll end my exhortation after dinner.

GRATIANO

You don't look well, Antonio. You're taking things too seriously. People with too much invested in the world always get hurt. I'm telling you, you don't look like yourself.

ANTONIO

For me the world is just the world, Gratiano—a stage where every person has a part to play. I play a sad one.

GRATIANO

Then I'll play the happy fool and get laugh lines on my face. I'd rather overload my liver with wine than starve my heart by denying myself fun. Why should any living man sit still like a statue? Why should he sleep when he's awake? Why should he get ulcers from being crabby all the time? I love you, and I'm telling you this because I care about you, Antonio there are men who always look serious. Their faces never move or show any expression, like stagnant ponds covered with scum. They're silent and stern, and they think they're wise and deep, important and respectable. When they talk, they think everybody else should keep quiet, and that even dogs should stop barking. I know a lot of men like that, Antonio. The only reason they're considered wise is because they don't say anything. I'm sure if they ever opened their mouths, everyone would see what fools they are. I'll talk to you more about this some other time. In the meantime, cheer up. Don't go around looking so glum. That's my opinion, but what do I know? I'm a fool.—Let's go, Lorenzo.—Goodbye for now. I'll finish my lecture after dinner.

LORENZO

105   Well, we will leave you then till dinnertime.
I must be one of these same dumb wise men,
For Gratiano never lets me speak.

GRATIANO

Well, keep me company but two years more,
Thou shalt not know the sound of thine own tongue.

ANTONIO

110   Farewell. I'll grow a talker for this gear.

GRATIANO

Thanks, i' faith, for silence is only commendable
In a neat's tongue dried and a maid not vendible.

Exeunt GRATIANO *and* LORENZO

ANTONIO

Is that any thing now?

BASSANIO

Gratiano speaks an infinite deal of nothing, more than
115   any man in all Venice. His reasons are as two grains of
wheat hid in two bushels of chaff—you shall seek all day
ere you find them, and when you have them they are not
worth the search.

ANTONIO

Well, tell me now what lady is the same
120   To whom you swore a secret pilgrimage,
That you today promised to tell me of?

BASSANIO

'Tis not unknown to you, Antonio,
How much I have disabled mine estate,
By something showing a more swelling port
125   Than my faint means would grant continuance.
Nor do I now make moan to be abridged
From such a noble rate. But my chief care

LORENZO

All right, we'll see you at dinnertime. I must be one of these silent so-called wise men Gratiano's talking about, because he never lets me get a word in.

GRATIANO

If you hang around me for two more years, you'll forget the sound of your own voice. I won't ever let you speak.

ANTONIO

Goodbye. After that lecture of yours, I'll start talking a lot.

GRATIANO

Thank you. The only tongues that should be silent are ox-tongues on a dinner plate and those that belong to old maids.

GRATIANO *and* LORENZO *exit.*

ANTONIO

Is he right?

BASSANIO

Gratiano talks more nonsense than any other man in Venice. His point is always like a needle in a haystack—you look for it all day, and when you find it you realize it wasn't worth the trouble.

ANTONIO

So, who's this girl, the one you said you were going to take a special trip for? You promised to tell me.

BASSANIO

Antonio, you know how bad my finances have been lately. I've been living way beyond my means. Don't get me wrong, I'm not complaining about having to cut back.

Is to come fairly off from the great debts
Wherein my time something too prodigal
130   Hath left me gaged. To you, Antonio,
I owe the most in money and in love,
And from your love I have a warranty
To unburden all my plots and purposes
How to get clear of all the debts I owe.

ANTONIO
135   I pray you, good Bassanio, let me know it.
And if it stand, as you yourself still do,
Within the eye of honor, be assured
My purse, my person, my extremest means
Lie all unlocked to your occasions.

BASSANIO
140   In my school days, when I had lost one shaft,
I shot his fellow of the selfsame flight
The selfsame way with more advisèd watch
To find the other forth—and by adventuring both,
I oft found both. I urge this childhood proof
145   Because what follows is pure innocence.
I owe you much, and, like a willful youth,
That which I owe is lost. But if you please
To shoot another arrow that self way
Which you did shoot the first, I do not doubt,
150   As I will watch the aim, or to find both
Or bring your latter hazard back again
And thankfully rest debtor for the first.

ANTONIO
You know me well, and herein spend but time
To wind about my love with circumstance.
155   And out of doubt you do me now more wrong
In making question of my uttermost
Than if you had made waste of all I have.
Then do but say to me what I should do
That in your knowledge may by me be done,
160   And I am pressed unto it. Therefore speak.

I just want to be honorable and pay off the big debts that piled up when I was living the high life. I'm in debt to many people, and I owe most to you, Antonio—both money and gratitude. And because you care about me, I know you'll let me tell you my plan to clear all my debts.

ANTONIO

Please let me know your plan, Bassanio. As long as it's honorable, you can be sure that I'll let you use all my money and do everything I can to help you.

BASSANIO

Back when I was a schoolboy, if I lost an arrow I would try to find it by shooting another arrow in the same direction, watching the second arrow more carefully than I had the first. By risking the second arrow, I'd often get both of them back. I'm telling you this story for a reason. I owe you a lot, and like a spoiled kid I've lost what I owe you. But if you'd be willing to shoot another arrow the same way you shot the first, I'll watch your arrow more carefully this time. Either we'll get back all the money I owe you, or else we'll get back what you lend me this time, and I'll just owe you what I already owe you.

ANTONIO

You know me better than that. You're wasting your breath. All of this talk means you have doubts about my friendship. That's worse than if you bankrupted me. Just tell me what to do, and I'll do it. Tell me.

BASSANIO
In Belmont is a lady richly left,
And she is fair and—fairer than that word—
Of wondrous virtues. Sometimes from her eyes
I did receive fair speechless messages.
165   Her name is Portia, nothing undervalued
To Cato's daughter, Brutus' Portia.
Nor is the wide world ignorant of her worth,
For the four winds blow in from every coast
Renownèd suitors, and her sunny locks
170   Hang on her temples like a golden fleece,
Which makes her seat of Belmont Colchos' strand,
And many Jasons come in quest of her.
O my Antonio, had I but the means
To hold a rival place with one of them,
175   I have a mind presages me such thrift
That I should questionless be fortunate!

ANTONIO
Thou know'st that all my fortunes are at sea.
Neither have I money nor commodity
To raise a present sum. Therefore go forth,
180   Try what my credit can in Venice do—
That shall be racked even to the uttermost
To furnish thee to Belmont, to fair Portia.
Go presently inquire, and so will I,
Where money is, and I no question make
185   To have it of my trust or for my sake.

Exeunt

BASSANIO

There's a girl in Belmont who's inherited a huge amount of money, and she's beautiful and—even better—she's a good person. I think she likes me. Sometimes the expression on her face tells me she likes me. Her name is Portia. She's as rich as that famous Roman heroine Portia, the daughter of Cato and wife of Brutus. Her wealth is world-famous. Famous and important men have come in from all over the world to try to marry her. The hair that hangs down on her forehead is like gold, calling every adventurer to Belmont like a gold rush. Antonio, if I only had enough money to hold my own against those suitors, I know I could win her!

ANTONIO

You know right now all my money's tied up in that cargo that's still at sea. I can't give you the cash you need because I don't have it. But go ahead and charge things to me on credit, as much credit as I can get in Venice. I'll use all my lines of credit to help you get to Belmont, to Portia. Go see who will lend money, and I'll do the same. I'm sure I can get something either as a business loan, or as a personal favor.

They exit.

ACT ONE, Scene 2

Enter PORTIA *and* NERISSA

PORTIA
By my troth, Nerissa, my little body is aweary of this great
world.

NERISSA
You would be, sweet madam, if your miseries were in the
same abundance as your good fortunes are. And yet for
aught I see, they are as sick that surfeit with too much as
they that starve with nothing. It is no mean happiness,
therefore, to be seated in the mean. Superfluity comes
sooner by white hairs, but competency lives longer.

PORTIA
Good sentences, and well pronounced.

NERISSA
They would be better if well followed.

PORTIA
If to do were as easy as to know what were good to do,
chapels had been churches and poor men's cottages
princes' palaces. It is a good divine that follows his own
instructions. I can easier teach twenty what were good to
be done than to be one of the twenty to follow mine
own teaching. The brain may devise laws for the blood,
but a hot temper leaps o'er a cold decree. Such a hare is
madness the youth—to skip o'er the meshes of good
counsel the cripple. But this reasoning is not in the
fashion to choose me a husband. O me, the word
"choose!" I may neither choose whom I would nor refuse
whom I dislike—so is the will of a living daughter curbed
by the will of a dead father. Is it not hard, Nerissa, that I
cannot choose one nor refuse none?

ACT ONE, Scene 2

PORTIA *and* NERISSA *enter.*

PORTIA

Oh Nerissa, my poor little body is tired of this great big world.

NERISSA

You'd be tired, madam, if you had bad luck rather than wealth and good luck. But as far as I can tell, people with too much suffer as much as people with nothing. The best way to be happy is to be in between. When you have too much you get old sooner, but having just enough helps you live longer.

PORTIA

Good point, and well said.

NERISSA

It would be better if you actually applied it to your life.

PORTIA

You think it's that easy? If doing good deeds were as easy as knowing how to do them, then everyone would be better off. Small chapels would be big churches, and poor men's cottages would be princes' palaces. It takes a good priest to practice what he preaches. For me, it's easier to lecture twenty people on how to be good than to be the one person out of twenty who actually does good things. The brain can tell the heart what to do, but what does it matter? Cold rules don't matter when you've got a hot temper. Young people are like frisky young rabbits, and good advice is like a crippled old man trying to catch them. But thinking like this won't help me choose a husband. Oh, the word "choose" is strange! I can't choose who I like, or refuse who I dislike. I'm a living daughter still controlled by the wishes of her dead father. Isn't it a pain that I can't choose or refuse anyone, Nerissa?

NERISSA

25 Your father was ever virtuous, and holy men at their death
have good inspirations. Therefore the lottery that he hath
devised in these three chests of gold, silver, and lead,
whereof who chooses his meaning chooses you, will no
doubt never be chosen by any rightly but one who shall
30 rightly love. But what warmth is there in your affection
towards any of these princely suitors that are already
come?

PORTIA

I pray thee, overname them. And as thou namest them, I
will describe them. And according to my description,
35 level at my affection.

NERISSA

First, there is the Neapolitan prince.

PORTIA

Ay, that's a colt indeed, for he doth nothing but talk of his
horse, and he makes it a great appropriation to his own
good parts that he can shoe him himself. I am much afeard
40 my lady his mother played false with a smith.

NERISSA

Then there is the County Palatine.

PORTIA

He doth nothing but frown, as who should say, "An you
will not have me, choose." He hears merry tales and
smiles not. I fear he will prove the weeping philosopher
45 when he grows old, being so full of unmannerly sadness
in his youth. I had rather be married to a death's-head
with a bone in his mouth than to either of these. God
defend me from these two!

NERISSA

How say you by the French lord, Monsieur le Bon?

NERISSA

Your father was an extremely moral man, and religious people get odd ideas on their deathbeds. Your father's idea was to have a game with three boxes. The suitor who can figure out whether to pick the gold, silver, or lead box will solve your father's riddle—and that suitor's the man for you. No one will ever choose the right box who doesn't deserve your love. But tell me. Do you like any of the princely suitors who've come?

PORTIA

Run through the list. As you name them I'll describe them for you, and from my descriptions you can guess how I feel toward them.

NERISSA

Well, first there was the prince from Naples.

PORTIA

Ah, yes, that stallion. All he talks about is his horse. He thinks it's a great credit to his character that he can shoe a horse all by himself. I'm afraid his mother may have had an affair with a blacksmith.

NERISSA

Then there's the Count Palatine.

PORTIA

He does nothing but frown, as if he wants to say, "If you don't want me, I don't care." He doesn't even smile when he hears funny stories. If he's so sad and solemn when he's young, I can only imagine how much he'll cry as an old man. No, I'd rather be married to a skull with a bone in its mouth than to either of those men. God protect me from these two!

NERISSA

What did you think about that French lord, Monsieur le Bon?

PORTIA

50 God made him and therefore let him pass for a man. In truth, I know it is a sin to be a mocker, but he!—why, he hath a horse better than the Neapolitan's, a better bad habit of frowning than the Count Palatine. He is every man in no man. If a throstle sing, he falls straight a-

55 capering. He will fence with his own shadow. If I should marry him, I should marry twenty husbands. If he would despise me I would forgive him, for if he love me to madness I shall never requite him.

NERISSA

What say you then to Falconbridge, the young baron of

60 England?

PORTIA

You know I say nothing to him, for he understands not me, nor I him. He hath neither Latin, French, nor Italian, and you will come into the court and swear that I have a poor pennyworth in the English. He is a proper man's

65 picture, but alas, who can converse with a dumb show? How oddly he is suited! I think he bought his doublet in Italy, his round hose in France, his bonnet in Germany, and his behavior everywhere.

NERISSA

What think you of the Scottish lord, his neighbor?

PORTIA

70 That he hath a neighborly charity in him, for he borrowed a box of the ear of the Englishman and swore he would pay him again when he was able. I think the Frenchman became his surety and sealed under for another.

PORTIA

We might as well call him a man, since God created him. No, I know it's bad to make fun of people, but still! His horse is better than the Neapolitan's and he frowns more than the Count Palatine. He was trying to outdo everyone so much that you couldn't tell who he was. He started dancing every time a bird sang, and he was so eager to show off his fencing that he'd fight with his own shadow. If I married him, I might as well as marry twenty husbands, because he's like twenty men all rolled into one! I'd understand it if he hated me, since even if he loved me desperately, I'd never be able to love him back.

NERISSA

What about Falconbridge, that young English baron?

PORTIA

I have no opinion about him. We don't talk because we don't understand each other. He doesn't speak Latin, French, or Italian, and you know how little English I speak. He's great-looking, but how can you talk to someone who doesn't speak your language? He was dressed so oddly too! I think he got his jacket in Italy, his tights in France, his hat in Germany, and his behavior everywhere.

NERISSA

What do you think of his neighbor, the Scottish lord?

PORTIA

I think he's very forgiving, since he let the Englishman slap him on the ear without hitting him back. Rather than defend himself, he just threatened to pay the Englishman back later. Then the Frenchman promised to help the Scot pay the Englishman back, and added a slap of his own.

NERISSA

How like you the young German, the Duke of Saxony's
75   nephew?

PORTIA

Very vilely in the morning, when he is sober, and most
vilely in the afternoon, when he is drunk. When he is best
he is a little worse than a man, and when he is worst he is
little better than a beast. And the worst fall that ever fell,
80   I hope I shall make shift to go without him.

NERISSA

If he should offer to choose and choose the right casket,
you should refuse to perform your father's will if you
should refuse to accept him.

PORTIA

Therefore, for fear of the worst, I pray thee, set a deep
85   glass of rhenish wine on the contrary casket, for if the
devil be within and that temptation without, I know he
will choose it. I will do any thing, Nerissa, ere I'll be
married to a sponge.

NERISSA

You need not fear, lady, the having any of these lords.
90   They have acquainted me with their determinations,
which is indeed to return to their home and to trouble you
with no more suit unless you may be won by some other
sort than your father's imposition depending on the
caskets.

PORTIA

If I live to be as old as Sibylla, I will die as chaste as Diana
95   unless I be obtained by the manner of my father's will. I
am glad this parcel of wooers are so reasonable, for there
is not one among them but I dote on his very absence.
And I pray God grant them a fair departure.

NERISSA

Do you not remember, lady, in your father's time a
100   Venetian, a scholar and a soldier, that came hither in
company of the Marquess of Montferrat?

NERISSA

How did you like the young German, the duke of Saxony's nephew?

PORTIA

He's pretty awful in the morning when he's sobering up, and even worse in the afternoon when he's drunk. At his best he's a little less than a man, and at his worst he's little more than an animal. If we got married and he tragically met his demise, I'm sure I could find a way to go on without him.

NERISSA

If he offers to play the game and chooses the right box, but then you reject him, you'll be disobeying your father's last wishes.

PORTIA

I know. So please put a nice big glass of white wine on the wrong box. I know he'll get tempted and choose that one. I'll do anything rather than marry a drunk, Nerissa.

NERISSA

You don't have to worry about any of these lords, my lady. They've all told me what they want, which is to go back home and give up on you—unless there was some other way to win you than your father's pick-the-box test.

PORTIA

I'll die an old maid unless I can be won according to the rules set by my father's will. I'm glad these suitors are sensible enough to stay away. The only thing I like about them is that they're not there. I wish them all safe trips home.

NERISSA

Do you remember a Venetian scholar and soldier who accompanied the marquess of Montferrat here once when your father was still alive?

PORTIA
> Yes, yes, it was Bassanio—as I think he was so called.

NERISSA
> True, madam. He, of all the men that ever my foolish eyes
105   looked upon, was the best deserving a fair lady.

PORTIA
> I remember him well, and I remember him worthy of thy
> praise.

Enter a SERVINGMAN

> How now, what news?

SERVANT
> The four strangers seek for you, madam, to take their
110   leave. And there is a forerunner come from a fifth, the
> Prince of Morocco, who brings word the prince his
> master will be here tonight.

PORTIA
> If I could bid the fifth welcome with so good a heart as I
> can bid the other four farewell, I should be glad of his
115   approach. If he have the condition of a saint and the
> complexion of a devil, I had rather he should shrive me
> than wive me. Come, Nerissa.—*(to* SERVANT*)* Sirrah, go
> before. Whiles we shut the gates upon one wooer
> Another knocks at the door.

Exeunt

PORTIA

Yes, yes, that was Bassanio. I think that was his name.

NERISSA

Yes, madam, that's the one. He deserves a beautiful wife more than all the other men I've ever seen.

PORTIA

I remember him well, and my memory tells me that he deserves your praise.

A SERVANT *enters.*

Hello, do you have any news?

SERVANT

The four suitors are looking for you so they can say goodbye, madam. And there's a messenger representing a fifth one, the prince of Morocco, who says the prince will be here tonight.

PORTIA

If I could say hello to the fifth one as happily as I'll say goodbye to the first four, I'd be very happy he's coming. If he's as good as a saint but is black like a devil, I'd rather he hear my confession than marry me. Let's go, Nerissa.—*(to the* SERVANT*)* Go ahead. As soon as we shut the door on one suitor, another one starts knocking.

They exit.

ACT ONE

ACT ONE, Scene 3

Enter BASSANIO *and* SHYLOCK

SHYLOCK
Three thousand ducats, well.

BASSANIO
Ay, sir, for three months.

SHYLOCK
For three months, well.

BASSANIO
For the which, as I told you, Antonio shall be bound.

SHYLOCK
5   Antonio shall become bound, well.

BASSANIO
May you stead me? Will you pleasure me? Shall I know
your answer?

SHYLOCK
Three thousand ducats for three months, and Antonio
bound.

BASSANIO
10   Your answer to that?

SHYLOCK
Antonio is a good man.

BASSANIO
Have you heard any imputation to the contrary?

SHYLOCK
Ho, no, no, no, no. My meaning in saying he is a good
man is to have you understand me that he is sufficient. Yet
15   his means are in supposition. He hath an argosy bound to
Tripolis, another to the Indies. I understand moreover,
upon the Rialto, he hath a third at Mexico, a fourth for
England, and other ventures he hath squandered abroad.

ACT ONE, Scene 3

BASSANIO *and* SHYLOCK *enter.*

SHYLOCK

Three thousand ducats, hmmm.

BASSANIO

Yes, for three months.

SHYLOCK

For three months, hmmm.

BASSANIO

As I said before, Antonio will guarantee the loan. If I default, he'll pay you.

SHYLOCK

Antonio will guarantee it, hmmm.

BASSANIO

Can you help me? What's your answer?

SHYLOCK

Three thousand ducats for three months, and Antonio will guarantee it.

BASSANIO

Your answer?

SHYLOCK

Antonio's a good man.

BASSANIO

Have you heard anything to the contrary?

SHYLOCK

What? No, no, no, no. What I meant in saying he's a good man is that he has enough money to guarantee the loan. But his investments are uncertain right now. He has one ship bound for Tripoli, another heading for the Indies. What's more, people at the Rialto tell me he has a third ship in Mexico, and a fourth in England, as well as other business ventures throughout the world.

The Rialto is the business district of Venice, where the merchants meet.

But ships are but boards, sailors but men. There be land
20   rats and water rats, water thieves and land thieves—I
mean pirates—and then there is the peril of waters,
winds, and rocks. The man is notwithstanding sufficient.
Three thousand ducats—I think I may take his bond.

BASSANIO
Be assured you may.

SHYLOCK
25   I will be assured I may, and that I may be assured,
I will bethink me. May I speak with Antonio?

BASSANIO
If it please you to dine with us.

SHYLOCK
Yes—to smell pork, to eat of the habitation which your
prophet the Nazarite conjured the devil into. I will buy
30   with you, sell with you, talk with you, walk with you, and
so following, but I will not eat with you, drink with you,
nor pray with you. What news on the Rialto? Who is he
comes here?

Enter ANTONIO

BASSANIO
This is Signor Antonio.

SHYLOCK
35   *(aside)* How like a fawning publican he looks!
I hate him for he is a Christian,
But more for that in low simplicity
He lends out money gratis and brings down
The rate of usance here with us in Venice.
40   If I can catch him once upon the hip,
I will feed fat the ancient grudge I bear him.
He hates our sacred nation, and he rails,
Even there where merchants most do congregate,
On me, my bargains and my well-won thrift,

But ships are just fragile boards, and sailors are just men. There are rats and thieves and pirates—not to mention storms, winds, and rocks. Anything could happen. But in spite of all this, the man is still wealthy enough. Three thousand ducats—I think I can let him guarantee your loan.

BASSANIO

I assure you he can.

SHYLOCK

I *will* be sure he can, before I make the loan. And I'll think of a way to be sure. Can I speak with Antonio?

BASSANIO

If you like, you can dine with us.

SHYLOCK

Any meat from pigs (like pork or bacon) is forbidden by Jewish dietary law.

Oh yes—to smell pork? I don't think so! Your prophet Jesus sent the devil into a herd of pigs. I'm not going to eat that. I'll buy with you, sell with you, talk with you, walk with you, and so on, but I won't eat with you, drink with you, or pray with you. Any news on the Rialto? Who's that?

ANTONIO *enters.*

BASSANIO

This is Signor Antonio.

SHYLOCK

(to himself) He looks just like a guy who's robbed me but now comes to beg me for a favor! I hate him because he's a Christian. But more than that, I hate him because he stupidly lends money without interest, which lowers the interest rates here in Venice. If I can just get the upper hand of him once, I'll satisfy my old grudge against him. He hates Jews. Even at the Rialto he's always complaining about me and my negotiating and my hard-earned profits, which he

45   Which he calls "interest." Cursèd be my tribe
   If I forgive him!

BASSANIO
   Shylock, do you hear?

SHYLOCK
   I am debating of my present store,
   And by the near guess of my memory
50   I cannot instantly raise up the gross
   Of full three thousand ducats. What of that?
   Tubal, a wealthy Hebrew of my tribe,
   Will furnish me. But soft! How many months
   Do you desire?
   (to ANTONIO*)*
         Rest you fair, good signor.
55   Your worship was the last man in our mouths.

ANTONIO
   Shylock, albeit I neither lend nor borrow
   By taking nor by giving of excess,
   Yet to supply the ripe wants of my friend,
   I'll break a custom.
   (to BASSANIO*)*
        Is he yet possessed
60   How much ye would?

SHYLOCK
   Ay, ay, three thousand ducats.

ANTONIO
   And for three months.

SHYLOCK
   I had forgot—three months.
   (to BASSANIO*)*
         You told me so.
   (to ANTONIO*)*
   Well then, your bond, and let me see—But hear you,
65   Methought you said you neither lend nor borrow
   Upon advantage.

calls "interest." It would an insult to Jews everywhere to forgive that man!

BASSANIO

Shylock, are you listening?

SHYLOCK

I'm thinking about how much cash I have on hand. If I remember correctly, I can't raise the entire three thousand ducats immediately. But so what? Tubal, a wealthy Jew I know, will supply me with the cash. But wait a minute! How many months do you want? *(to* ANTONIO*)* Oh, hello, how are you, signor? We were just talking about you.

ANTONIO

Shylock, although I never lend or borrow with interest, I'm willing to break that habit to help a friend in need. *(to* BASSANIO*)* Does he know how much you need?

SHYLOCK

Oh yes, three thousand ducats.

ANTONIO

For three months.

SHYLOCK

Yes, I forgot—three months. *(to* BASSANIO*)* You told me that. *(to* ANTONIO*)* Now then, about your guarantee. Let me see—but listen, Antonio, I thought you said you don't lend or borrow with interest.

ANTONIO
     I do never use it.

SHYLOCK
  When Jacob grazed his uncle Laban's sheep—
  This Jacob from our holy Abram was,
  As his wise mother wrought in his behalf,
70 The third possessor, ay, he was the third—

ANTONIO
  And what of him? Did he take interest?

SHYLOCK
  No, not take interest—not as you would say
  Directly interest. Mark what Jacob did:
  When Laban and himself were compromised
75 That all the eanlings which were streaked and pied
  Should fall as Jacob's hire, the ewes, being rank,
  In the end of autumn turnèd to the rams.
  And when the work of generation was
  Between these woolly breeders in the act,
80 The skillful shepherd peeled me certain wands.
  And in the doing of the deed of kind
  He stuck them up before the fulsome ewes,
  Who then conceiving did in eaning time
  Fall parti-colored lambs—and those were Jacob's.
85 This was a way to thrive, and he was blessed.
  And thrift is blessing, if men steal it not.

ANTONIO
  This was a venture, sir, that Jacob served for—
  A thing not in his power to bring to pass
  But swayed and fashioned by the hand of heaven.
90 Was this inserted to make interest good?
  Or is your gold and silver ewes and rams?

SHYLOCK
  I cannot tell: I make it breed as fast.
  But note me, signor—

ANTONIO

That's right. That's not how I do business.

SHYLOCK

When Jacob took care of his uncle Laban's sheep— Jacob was the heir to his grandfather Abraham's birthright, because his mother cleverly arranged for her husband Isaac to make Jacob his heir—

ANTONIO

What's your point? Did he charge interest?

SHYLOCK

No, he didn't charge interest—not in your sense of the word. But listen to what Jacob did. When he and Laban agreed that all the spotted lambs would be Jacob's pay, it was the end of autumn, when the sheep were starting to mate. Because newborns look like whatever their mother sees during mating, he stuck some spotted branches into the ground right in front of the sheep, who saw them while they mated. The mothers later gave birth to spotted lambs, all of which went to Jacob. That was his way of expanding his business, and it worked. My point is that profit is a blessing, as long as you don't steal to get it.

Shylock uses a story of Jacob from Genesis 30:25–43 to defend his practice of charging interest.

ANTONIO

That business venture you're referring to happened because God made it happen like that. Jacob didn't have any control over what happened. Are you saying this story proves that charging interest makes sense? That your interest payments are like Jacob's sheep?

SHYLOCK

I can hardly tell the difference; I make my money multiply as fast as those sheep. But listen to me, signor—

ANTONIO
Mark you this, Bassanio,
The devil can cite Scripture for his purpose.
95　An evil soul producing holy witness
Is like a villain with a smiling cheek,
A goodly apple rotten at the heart.
Oh, what a goodly outside falsehood hath!

SHYLOCK
Three thousand ducats—'tis a good round sum.
100　Three months from twelve, then. Let me see. The rate—

ANTONIO
Well, Shylock, shall we be beholding to you?

SHYLOCK
Signor Antonio, many a time and oft
In the Rialto you have rated me
About my moneys and my usances.
105　Still have I borne it with a patient shrug,
For sufferance is the badge of all our tribe.
You call me misbeliever, cutthroat dog,
And spet upon my Jewish gaberdine—
And all for use of that which is mine own.
110　Well then, it now appears you need my help.
Go to, then! You come to me and you say,
"Shylock, we would have moneys." You say so!—
You, that did void your rheum upon my beard
And foot me as you spurn a stranger cur
115　Over your threshold! Moneys is your suit.
What should I say to you? Should I not say,
"Hath a dog money? Is it possible
A cur can lend three thousand ducats?" Or
Shall I bend low and in a bondman's key
120　With bated breath and whispering humbleness
Say this:

ANTONIO

Watch out, Bassanio. The devil can quote Scripture for his own use. An evil soul using a holy story is like a criminal who smiles at you. He looks like a good apple but he's rotten at the core. Oh, liars can look so honest!

SHYLOCK

Three thousand ducats. That's a nice even sum. Three months from twelve months of the year. Let me see. The interest rate will be—

ANTONIO

Well, Shylock? Are you going to loan us the money?

SHYLOCK

Signor Antonio, you've often insulted my money and my business practices in the Rialto. I have always just shrugged and put up with it because Jews are good at suffering. You called me a heathen, a dirty dog, and you spit on my Jewish clothes. And all because I use my own money to make a profit. And now it looks like you need my help. All right then. You come to me saying, "Shylock, we need money." You say that!—even though you spat on my beard and kicked me like you'd kick a stray mutt out your front door. And now you're asking for money. What can I tell you? Shouldn't I say, "Does a dog have money? Is it possible for a mutt to lend three thousand ducats?" Or should I bend down low, and in a humble and submissive voice say:

"Fair sir, you spet on me on Wednesday last;
You spurned me such a day; another time
You called me 'dog'—and for these courtesies
125 I'll lend you thus much moneys?"

ANTONIO
I am as like to call thee so again,
To spet on thee again, to spurn thee too.
If thou wilt lend this money, lend it not
As to thy friends, for when did friendship take
130 A breed for barren metal of his friend?
But lend it rather to thine enemy,
Who, if he break, thou mayst with better face
Exact the penalty.

SHYLOCK
       Why, look you how you storm!
I would be friends with you and have your love,
135 Forget the shames that you have stained me with,
Supply your present wants and take no doit
Of usance for my moneys—and you'll not hear me!
This is kind I offer.

BASSANIO
         This were kindness.

SHYLOCK
This kindness will I show.
140 Go with me to a notary, seal me there
Your single bond, and—in a merry sport—
If you repay me not on such a day,
In such a place, such sum or sums as are
Expressed in the condition, let the forfeit
145 Be nominated for an equal pound
Of your fair flesh, to be cut off and taken
In what part of your body pleaseth me.

ANTONIO
Content, in faith. I'll seal to such a bond,
And say there is much kindness in the Jew.

"Sir, last Wednesday you spit on me. You insulted me on this day, and another time you called me a dog. And out of gratitude for these favors, I'll be happy to lend you the money?"

ANTONIO

I'll probably call you those names again and spit on you, and reject you again too. If you're going to lend us this money, don't lend it to us as if we were your friends. When did friends charge interest? Instead, lend it to me as your enemy. If your enemy goes bankrupt, it's easier for you to take your penalty from him.

SHYLOCK

Look at you getting all riled up! I want to be friends with you, and forget all the times you've embarrassed and humiliated me. I want to give you what you need, and not charge a penny of interest—but you won't listen to me! I'm making a kind offer—zero percent financing.

BASSANIO

That really would be kind.

SHYLOCK

I'll show you how kind I am. Come with me to a notary and we'll make it official. And let's add a little clause just for a joke. If you don't repay me on the day we agree on, in the place we name, for the sum of money fixed in our contract, your penalty will be a pound of your pretty flesh, to be cut off and taken out of whatever part of your body I like.

ANTONIO

It's a deal. I'll agree to those terms and even say that Jews are nice.

BASSANIO

150   You shall not seal to such a bond for me!
I'll rather dwell in my necessity.

ANTONIO

Why, fear not, man. I will not forfeit it.
Within these two months—that's a month before
This bond expires—I do expect return
155   Of thrice three times the value of this bond.

SHYLOCK

O Father Abram, what these Christians are,
Whose own hard dealings teaches them suspect
The thoughts of others!—Pray you, tell me this:
If he should break his day, what should I gain
160   By the exaction of the forfeiture?
A pound of man's flesh taken from a man
Is not so estimable, profitable neither,
As flesh of muttons, beefs, or goats. I say,
To buy his favor I extend this friendship.
165   If he will take it, so. If not, adieu.
And for my love I pray you wrong me not.

ANTONIO

Yes, Shylock, I will seal unto this bond.

SHYLOCK

Then meet me forthwith at the notary's.
Give him direction for this merry bond,
170   And I will go and purse the ducats straight,
See to my house left in the fearful guard
Of an unthrifty knave, and presently
I will be with you.

ANTONIO

Hie thee, gentle Jew.

Exit SHYLOCK

175   The Hebrew will turn Christian. He grows kind.

BASSANIO

No, you can't sign a contract like that for me! I'd rather go without the money.

ANTONIO

Don't worry about it, man, I won't have to pay any penalty. In two months—a month before this loan is due—I expect to earn thrice three times that much from my investments.

SHYLOCK

Oh father Abraham, what kind of people are these Christians? Their own meanness teaches them to suspect other people! —Please tell me this. If he fails to repay me by the deadline, what would I get out of such a penalty? A pound of human flesh taken isn't even as valuable as a pound of mutton or beef. I'm just offering this as a favor to a friend. If he agrees, great. If not, goodbye. And I hope you won't think badly of me.

ANTONIO

Yes, Shylock, I'll sign the contract and agree to its terms.

SHYLOCK

Then meet me right away at the notary's. Give him the instructions for our amusing little contract, and I'll go get the money for you right away. I need to check in at home first, because one of my careless servants is in charge right now. I'll see you soon.

ANTONIO

Hurry up, my Jewish friend.

SHYLOCK exits.

He's so kind you'd think the Jew is turning Christian.

ACT ONE

BASSANIO
    I like not fair terms and a villain's mind.

ANTONIO
    Come on. In this there can be no dismay.
    My ships come home a month before the day.

Exeunt

BASSANIO

    I don't like it when a villain acts nice.

ANTONIO

    Come on, there's no reason to worry. My ships will come home a month before the money is due.

They exit.

ACT TWO

Scene 1

Flourish cornets
Enter the Prince of MOROCCO, *a tawny Moor all in white, and*
three or four followers accordingly, with PORTIA, NERISSA,
and their train

MOROCCO
Mislike me not for my complexion,
The shadowed livery of the burnished sun,
To whom I am a neighbor and near bred.
Bring me the fairest creature northward born,
5   Where Phoebus' fire scarce thaws the icicles,
And let us make incision for your love
To prove whose blood is reddest, his or mine.
I tell thee, lady, this aspect of mine
Hath feared the valiant. By my love I swear
10   The best-regarded virgins of our clime
Have loved it too. I would not change this hue
Except to steal your thoughts, my gentle queen.

PORTIA
In terms of choice I am not solely led
By nice direction of a maiden's eyes.
15   Besides, the lottery of my destiny
Bars me the right of voluntary choosing.
But if my father had not scanted me
And hedged me by his wit to yield myself
His wife who wins me by that means I told you,
20   Yourself, renownèd Prince, then stood as fair
As any comer I have looked on yet
For my affection.

ACT TWO

Scene 1

Trumpets play. The prince of MOROCCO, *a brown-skinned man dressed in all white, enters, followed by three or four servants dressed in costumes like his.* PORTIA, NERISSA, *and their* ATTENDANTS *enter.*

MOROCCO

Don't hold my skin color against me. I was born and raised in the sun, which is why I'm dark-skinned. But I'm as red-blooded as any man. Show me the best-looking person born in the freezing north, where the sun barely thaws the icicles. I'll win your love by cutting myself to prove to you I have redder blood than he does. I'm telling you, madam, my skin color has made brave men fear me and Moroccan girls love me. I wouldn't change it except to make you think of me, my darling queen.

PORTIA

Being good-looking isn't the only way to my heart, you know. I have other criteria for choosing a husband. Not that it matters, because the box test takes away my free choice anyway. But if my father hadn't restricted me like this—forcing me to marry whoever wins his test—then you'd have had as good a chance to marry me as any of the suitors I've met so far, prince.

MOROCCO
                              Even for that I thank you.
Therefore I pray you lead me to the caskets
To try my fortune. By this scimitar
25 That slew the Sophy and a Persian prince
That won three fields of Sultan Solyman,
I would o'erstare the sternest eyes that look,
Outbrave the heart most daring on the earth,
Pluck the young sucking cubs from the she-bear,
30 Yea, mock the lion when he roars for prey,
To win the lady. But, alas the while!
If Hercules and Lychas play at dice
Which is the better man, the greater throw
May turn by fortune from the weaker hand.
35 So is Alcides beaten by his page,
And so may I, blind fortune leading me,
Miss that which one unworthier may attain
And die with grieving.

PORTIA
                              You must take your chance,
And either not attempt to choose at all
40 Or swear before you choose, if you choose wrong
Never to speak to lady afterward
In way of marriage. Therefore be advised.

MOROCCO
Nor will not. Come, bring me unto my chance.

PORTIA
First, forward to the temple. After dinner
45 Your hazard shall be made.

MOROCCO
                              Good fortune then!—
To make me blessed or cursed'st among men.

Cornets

                                        Exeunt

MOROCCO

Thank you for saying that. Show me the caskets and let me try my luck. I swear by my sword, which killed the Shah of Persia and a Persian prince and defeated the Sultan Suleiman three times, that I would face the meanest-looking warriors on earth. I would act braver than the bravest man on earth. I would grab bear cubs from a ferocious mother bear, or tease a hungry lion— all of this in order to win your love, lady. But this is bad! If the hero Hercules and his servant Lychas rolled the dice, which would win? Not the greater hero. Just the one who happened to be luckier that time. And just as Hercules could be beaten by his servant, blind luck could make me lose this test and make someone worse than me win. If that happened, I'd die of sadness.

PORTIA

You have to take your chances. Either don't choose at all, or swear beforehand that if you choose incorrectly you'll never talk about marriage to any woman again. Think about it carefully.

MOROCCO

Fine, I swear I won't ever get married if I choose incorrectly. Let me take my chances.

PORTIA

Let's go to the temple first. You can take your chances after dinner.

MOROCCO

I'll try my luck then. I'll either be the luckiest or the unluckiest man alive.

Trumpets play.

They exit.

ACT TWO, Scene 2

Enter LAUNCELOT *the clown, alone*

LAUNCELOT

Certainly my conscience will serve me to run from this
Jew, my master. The fiend is at mine elbow and tempts
me, saying to me, "Gobbo," "Launcelot Gobbo," "Good
Launcelot," or "Good Gobbo," or "Good Launcelot
5   Gobbo"—"use your legs, take the start, run away." My
conscience says, "No. Take heed, honest Launcelot. Take
heed, honest Gobbo," or as aforesaid, "Honest Launcelot
Gobbo, do not run. Scorn running with thy heels." Well,
the most courageous fiend bids me pack. "Fia!" says the
10   fiend. "Away!" says the fiend. "For the heavens, rouse up
a brave mind," says the fiend, "and run." Well, my
conscience, hanging about the neck of my heart, says very
wisely to me, "My honest friend Launcelot, being an
honest man's son"—or rather an honest woman's son, for
15   indeed my father did something smack, something grow
to. He had a kind of taste.—Well, my conscience says,
"Launcelot, budge not." "Budge!" says the fiend.
"Budge not," says my conscience. "Conscience," say I,
"you counsel well." "Fiend," say I, "you counsel well."
20   To be ruled by my conscience I should stay with the Jew
my master, who, God bless the mark, is a kind of devil.
And to run away from the Jew I should be ruled by the
fiend, who, saving your reverence, is the devil himself.
Certainly the Jew is the very devil incarnation. And in my
25   conscience, my conscience is but a kind of hard
conscience, to offer to counsel me to stay with the Jew.
The fiend gives the more friendly counsel. I will run,
fiend. My heels are at your command. I will run.

Enter Old GOBBO *with a basket*

ACT TWO, Scene 2

LAUNCELOT *enters alone.*

LAUNCELOT
I'm sure I'll feel guilty if I run away from this Jew, my master. The devil's on my shoulder, tempting me. He's saying, "Gobbo," "Launcelot Gobbo," "Good Launcelot," or "Good Gobbo," or "Good Launcelot Gobbo"—"use your legs and run away." But my conscience says, "No, Launcelot, calm down, don't run away." The devil's urging me to leave. "Go away!" he says. "Run away! Be tough," says the devil, "and run!" But then my conscience, hanging around my heart, says very wisely to me, "My good friend Launcelot, you're a good boy, the son of an honest man," really, that should be the son of an honest woman, since my father cheated on my mother. Anyway, my conscience says, "Stay put." "Go," the devil says. "Don't go," says my conscience. "Conscience," I say, "you give good advice." "Devil," I say, "you give good advice." If I listened to my conscience, I'd stay with the Jew my master, who's a devil. But if I ran away from the Jew, I'd be following the advice of the devil, who's the very devil himself. Certainly the Jew is the devil incarnate, and my conscience is giving me a hard time by telling me to stay with the Jew. The devil's advice is nicer. I'll run, devil. Tell me to run, and I'll run.

GOBBO *enters with a basket.*

GOBBO

30 Master young man, you, I pray you, which is the way to Master Jew's?

LAUNCELOT

(aside) O heavens, this is my true-begotten father, who, being more than sand-blind—high-gravel blind—knows me not. I will try confusions with him.

GOBBO

35 Master young gentleman, I pray you, which is the way to Master Jew's?

LAUNCELOT

Turn up on your right hand at the next turning, but at the next turning of all on your left. Marry, at the very next turning turn of no hand, but turn down indirectly to the Jew's house.

GOBBO

40 By God's sonties, 'twill be a hard way to hit. Can you tell me whether one Launcelot that dwells with him, dwell with him or no?

LAUNCELOT

Talk you of young Master Launcelot? *(aside)* Mark me now. Now will I raise the waters.—Talk you of young 45 Master Launcelot?

GOBBO

No "master," sir, but a poor man's son. His father, though I say 't, is an honest exceeding poor man and, God be thanked, well to live.

LAUNCELOT

Well, let his father be what he will, we talk of young 50 Master Launcelot.

GOBBO

Your worship's friend and Launcelot, sir.

GOBBO

Excuse me, young man, how do I get to the Jew's residence?

LAUNCELOT

(to himself) Good heavens, it's my father. He doesn't recognize me because he's half-blind—or more than half-blind, somewhere between half-blind and totally blind. I'll play a little game with him.

GOBBO

Young man, excuse me, how do I get to the Jew's?

LAUNCELOT

Turn right at the next turn, but at the following turn, turn left. Oh, and then at the very next turn, don't turn left or right, but turn down and around to the Jew's house.

GOBBO

Good heavens, those are difficult directions. Can you tell me if a man named Launcelot, who lives with him, is still there?

LAUNCELOT

Are you talking about young Master Launcelot? *(speaking so no one else can hear)* Watch out, I'm going to pull a good prank here.—Is that who you're talking about?

GOBBO

He's not a "master," sir, he's just a poor man's son. His father, if I do say so myself, is an honest but very poor man, and, thank God, likely to live a long time.

LAUNCELOT

Well, his father can be whatever he wants to be. We're talking about young Master Launcelot.

GOBBO

Please don't call him that, sir. He's just Launcelot.

LAUNCELOT
But I pray you, ergo, old man, ergo, I beseech you, talk
you of young Master Launcelot?

GOBBO
Of Launcelot, an 't please your mastership.

LAUNCELOT
55   Ergo, Master Launcelot. Talk not of Master Launcelot,
Father, for the young gentleman, according to Fates and
Destinies and such odd sayings, the Sisters Three and
such branches of learning, is indeed deceased, or as you
would say in plain terms, gone to heaven.

GOBBO
60   Marry, God forbid! The boy was the very staff of my age,
my very prop.

LAUNCELOT
Do I look like a cudgel or a hovel-post, a staff or a prop?
Do you know me, Father?

GOBBO
Alack the day, I know you not, young gentleman. But I
65   pray you, tell me, is my boy, God rest his soul, alive or
dead?

LAUNCELOT
Do you not know me, Father?

GOBBO
Alack, sir, I am sand-blind. I know you not.

LAUNCELOT
Nay, indeed if you had your eyes, you might fail of the
70   knowing me. It is a wise father that knows his own child.
Well, old man, I will tell you news of your son. Give me
your blessing. Truth will come to light. Murder cannot be
hid long—a man's son may, but in the end truth will out.

LAUNCELOT

"Ergo" means "therefore" in Latin. Launcelot is using the word to prove he's an educated gentleman but seems to have no idea what it means.

But excuse me, *ergo*, old man, *ergo*, I'm asking you if you're talking about young Master Launcelot.

GOBBO

Yes, I'm talking about Launcelot, sir.

LAUNCELOT

Ergo, Master Launcelot. But please don't talk about Master Launcelot, old man. The young gentleman, submitting to the fates, the three sisters who control destiny, and other branches of learning like that, is deceased. Or, to put it in plain language, he's gone to heaven.

GOBBO

Oh, no. God forbid! The boy was going to support me in my old age!

LAUNCELOT

What am I, a cane? How could I support anyone? Don't you recognize me, father?

GOBBO

Heaven help me, I don't know you, sir. But please tell me, is my boy—God rest his soul—alive or dead?

LAUNCELOT

You really don't recognize me, father?

GOBBO

Sir, I'm half-blind. I don't know you.

LAUNCELOT

Even if you had your eyes, you still might not recognize me. It takes a wise father to know his own child. Well, old man, I'll tell you news of your son. Give me your blessing. The truth will come to light, and murder can't be hidden long—a man's son may hide, but truth will always come out.

GOBBO

Pray you, sir, stand up. I am sure you are not Launcelot,
75   my boy.

LAUNCELOT

Pray you, let's have no more fooling about it, but give me
your blessing. I am Launcelot, your boy that was, your
son that is, your child that shall be.

GOBBO

I cannot think you are my son.

LAUNCELOT

80   I know not what I shall think of that. But I am Launcelot,
the Jew's man, and I am sure Margery your wife is my
mother.

GOBBO

Her name is Margery, indeed. I'll be sworn, if thou be
Launcelot, thou art mine own flesh and blood. *(feels the*
85   *back of* LAUNCELOT*'s head)* Lord worshipped might he be,
what a beard hast thou got! Thou hast got more hair on
thy chin than Dobbin my fill-horse has on his tail.

LAUNCELOT

It should seem then that Dobbin's tail grows backward. I
am sure he had more hair of his tail than I have of my face
90   when I last saw him.

GOBBO

Lord, how art thou changed! How dost thou and thy
master agree? I have brought him a present. How 'gree
you now?

LAUNCELOT

Well, well, but for mine own part, as I have set up my rest
95   to run away, so I will not rest till I have run some ground.
My master's a very Jew. Give him a present. Give him a
halter. I am famished in his service. You may tell every
finger I have with my ribs. Father, I am glad you are come.
Give me your present to one Master Bassanio, who
100   indeed gives rare new liveries.

GOBBO

Please stand up! I'm sure you aren't Launcelot, my boy.

LAUNCELOT

Come on, quit fooling around. Give me your blessing. I'm Launcelot, who was your boy, is your son, and will be your child.

GOBBO

I can't believe you're my son.

LAUNCELOT

I don't know what to say to that, but the fact is I'm Launcelot, the Jew's servant, and Margery, your wife, is my mother.

GOBBO

Yes, you're right, her name is Margery. If you're Launcelot, then you're my own flesh and blood. *(feels the back of* LAUNCELOT'*s head)* My Lord, what a bushy beard you have! You've got more hair on your chin than Dobbin my horse has in his tail.

LAUNCELOT

Then Dobbin's tail must be growing backward. I'm sure he had more hair on his tail than I have on my face when I last saw him.

GOBBO

Lord, how you've changed! How are you and your master getting along? I've brought him a present. How are you?

LAUNCELOT

I'm all right. But I've decided to run away, and I can't wait to get going. My master's a total Jew. You're giving him a present? Give him a noose to hang himself. He's starving me to death. You can see my ribs so well you can count them. I'm glad you've come, father. Give me your present to give to Master Bassanio. He gives his servants beautiful new uniforms.

If I serve not him, I will run as far as God has any
ground.—O rare fortune! Here comes the man.—To
him, Father, for I am a Jew if I serve the Jew any longer.

Enter BASSANIO *with* LEONARDO *and another follower or two*

BASSANIO

(to a follower) You may do so, but let it be so hasted that
105   supper be ready at the farthest by five of the clock. See
these letters delivered, put the liveries to making, and
desire Gratiano to come anon to my lodging.

Exit follower

LAUNCELOT

To him, Father.

GOBBO

(to BASSANIO*)* God bless your worship!

BASSANIO

110   Gramercy! Wouldst thou aught with me?

GOBBO

Here's my son, sir, a poor boy—

LAUNCELOT

Not a poor boy, sir, but the rich Jew's man that would, sir,
as my father shall specify—

GOBBO

He hath a great infection, sir, as one would say, to serve—

LAUNCELOT

115   Indeed the short and the long is, I serve the Jew and have
a desire, as my father shall specify—

Launcelot uses the word "Jew" as a term of abuse here.

If I can't get a job with him, I'll run away to the ends of the earth.—Oh look, this is lucky, here comes Master Bassanio now.—Let's go talk to him, Father. If I work for the Jew any longer, you can just call me a Jew.

BASSANIO *enters with* LEONARDO *and an attendant or two.*

BASSANIO

(to an attendant) All right, go ahead. But do everything quickly. Supper must be ready at five at the latest. Make sure these letters get delivered, get the uniforms made, and tell Gratiano to come visit me soon.

The attendant exits.

LAUNCELOT

Go talk to him, father.

GOBBO

(to BASSANIO*)* God bless you, sir!

BASSANIO

Thank you. What do you want with me?

GOBBO

This is my son, sir. He's a poor boy—

LAUNCELOT

Not a poor boy, but the rich Jew's servant, who wants, as my father will explain—

GOBBO

He wants very much, sir, as one might say, to work for—

LAUNCELOT

To put it briefly, I work for the Jew, and I want, as my father will tell you—

GOBBO
    His master and he, saving your worship's reverence, are
    scarce cater-cousins—

LAUNCELOT
    To be brief, the very truth is that the Jew, having done me
120   wrong, doth cause me, as my father, being, I hope, an old
    man, shall frutify unto you—

GOBBO
    I have here a dish of doves that I would bestow upon your
    worship, and my suit is—

LAUNCELOT
    In very brief, the suit is impertinent to myself, as your
125   worship shall know by this honest old man—and though
    I say it, though old man, yet poor man, my father—

BASSANIO
    One speak for both. What would you?

LAUNCELOT
    Serve you, sir.

GOBBO
    That is the very defect of the matter, sir.

BASSANIO
130   I know thee well. Thou hast obtained thy suit.
    Shylock thy master spoke with me this day,
    And hath preferred thee, if it be preferment
    To leave a rich Jew's service, to become
    The follower of so poor a gentleman.

LAUNCELOT
135   The old proverb is very well parted between my master
    Shylock and you, sir—you have "the grace of God," sir,
    and he hath "enough."

BASSANIO
    Thou speak'st it well.—Go, father, with thy son.—
    Take leave of thy old master and inquire
140   My lodging out.—

GOBBO

He and his master aren't exactly friends—

LAUNCELOT

To be brief, the truth is that the Jew has done me wrong, and that forces me to—as my father, an old man, will inform you—

GOBBO

I have a present I'd like to give you, sir. And I want to request that—

LAUNCELOT

To make a long story short, the request is about me, as this good old man will tell you. Even though I'm his son and I'm the one saying it, this old man is a poor man—

BASSANIO

One of you do the talking. What do you want?

LAUNCELOT

To work for you, sir.

GOBBO

That's what we're trying to say, sir.

BASSANIO

I know who you are. You can have what you want. I spoke with your master Shylock today, and he recommended you to me. If you want to leave a rich Jew to work for a poor gentleman, you're welcome to.

LAUNCELOT

Do you know the old proverb "The grace of God is enough," sir? It could be divided between you and my boss Shylock—you have "the grace of God," and he has "enough."

BASSANIO

Nicely put.—Go with your son, old man.—Say goodbye to your old master and find your way to my house.

(to followers)

Give him a livery
More guarded than his fellows'. See it done.

LAUNCELOT

Father, in. I cannot get a service, no. I have ne'er a tongue
in my head. *(reading his own palm)* Well, if any man in
Italy have a fairer table which doth offer to swear upon a

145   book, I shall have good fortune. Go to, here's a simple line
of life. Here's a small trifle of wives. Alas, fifteen wives is
nothing! Eleven widows and nine maids is a simple
coming-in for one man. And then to 'scape drowning
thrice and to be in peril of my life with the edge of a

150   feather-bed—here are simple 'scapes. Well, if Fortune be
a woman, she's a good wench for this gear.—Father,
come. I'll take my leave of the Jew in the twinkling.

Exit LAUNCELOT *the clown with Old* GOBBO

BASSANIO

I pray thee, good Leonardo, think on this.
These things being bought and orderly bestowed,

155   Return in haste, for I do feast tonight
My best esteemed acquaintance. Hie thee, go.

LEONARDO

My best endeavours shall be done herein.

Enter GRATIANO

GRATIANO

(to LEONARDO*)* Where is your master?

LEONARDO

Yonder, sir, he walks.

Exit LEONARDO

(to attendants) Give him a uniform that's a little nicer than the others. Make sure it gets done.

LAUNCELOT

Father, go ahead. I can't get a job, can I? I can't talk well, no. *(reading his own palm)* If any man in Italy has a palm good enough to swear on a Bible with, it's me. I've got very good luck! Here's my life line. It shows a few wives—fifteen wives is nothing. Eleven widows and nine maids is a humble beginning for one man. It seems I'll almost drown three times, and my life will be in danger when I'm caught in bed with another man's wife! But these little lines are the escape routes I can take to get out of that one. If luck's a lady, she's good at this business. Father, let's go. I'll leave the Jew behind in the blink of an eye.

> **LAUNCELOT** *and* **GOBBO** *exit.*

BASSANIO

Please, Leonardo, think about this *(he hands him a piece of paper)*. These things have been bought and are ready. Hurry back here. I'm having dinner tonight with someone I greatly respect. Go now.

LEONARDO

I'll do my best.

> **GRATIANO** *enters.*

GRATIANO

(to **LEONARDO***)* Where's your master?

LEONARDO

He's walking over there, sir.

> **LEONARDO** *exits.*

GRATIANO
Signor Bassanio!

BASSANIO
                                        Gratiano!

GRATIANO
160   I have a suit to you.

BASSANIO
                                        You have obtained it.

GRATIANO
You must not deny me. I must go with you to Belmont.

BASSANIO
Why, then you must. But hear thee, Gratiano.
Thou art too wild, too rude and bold of voice—
Parts that become thee happily enough
165   And in such eyes as ours appear not faults.
But where thou art not known, why, there they show
Something too liberal. Pray thee, take pain
To allay with some cold drops of modesty
Thy skipping spirit, lest through thy wild behavior
170   I be misconst'red in the place I go to,
And lose my hopes.

GRATIANO
                                        Signor Bassanio, hear me.
If I do not put on a sober habit,
Talk with respect and swear but now and then,
Wear prayer books in my pocket, look demurely—
175   Nay more. While grace is saying, hood mine eyes
Thus with my hat, and sigh and say, "Amen"—
Use all the observance of civility
Like one well studied in a sad ostent
To please his grandam, never trust me more.

BASSANIO
180   Well, we shall see your bearing.

GRATIANO
Nay, but I bar tonight. You shall not gauge me
By what we do tonight.

GRATIANO

Signor Bassanio!

BASSANIO

Gratiano!

GRATIANO

I have a favor to ask.

BASSANIO

Anything.

GRATIANO

Don't say no. Let me go with you to Belmont.

BASSANIO

Well, if you have to go, you have to go. But listen to me, Gratiano. Sometimes you get a bit too wild, and you let your voice get a bit loud and rude. These things look good on you, of course, and to people like you and me there's nothing wrong with it. But in places where people don't know you, your behavior might seem too wild. Please, try to act a little more serious, or the people in Belmont will get the wrong impression about me, and your wildness will make me blow my chance with Portia.

GRATIANO

Listen, Signor Bassanio, there's nothing to worry about. I'll be solemn-looking, I'll talk with respect, and I'll only swear once in a while. I'll carry prayer books in my pocket and look sweet—even more. While grace is being said, I'll be modest and say "amen"—I'll watch my manners as if I'm trying to please my grandma. If I don't do all this, never trust me again.

BASSANIO

Well, we'll see how you act.

GRATIANO

Okay, but tonight doesn't count. You can't judge me based on what I do tonight.

BASSANIO
                              No, that were pity.
I would entreat you rather to put on
Your boldest suit of mirth, for we have friends
185   That purpose merriment. But fare you well.
I have some business.

GRATIANO
And I must to Lorenzo and the rest.
But we will visit you at supper time.

Exeunt severally

BASSANIO

No, it'd be a shame for you to act serious tonight. I'd rather see you having fun, because we have friends coming who want to have fun. Anyway, I have to say goodbye to you now. I've got some business to take care of.

GRATIANO

I have to join Lorenzo and the others, but we'll visit you at supper time.

They exit.

ACT TWO, Scene 3

Enter JESSICA *and* LAUNCELOT *the clown*

JESSICA
I am sorry thou wilt leave my father so.
Our house is hell, and thou, a merry devil,
Didst rob it of some taste of tediousness.
But fare thee well, there is a ducat for thee.
5　And Launcelot, soon at supper shalt thou see
Lorenzo, who is thy new master's guest.
Give him this letter.
(gives LAUNCELOT *a letter)*
　　　　　　　Do it secretly.
And so farewell. I would not have my father
See me in talk with thee.

LAUNCELOT
10　Adieu! Tears exhibit my tongue. Most beautiful pagan,
most sweet Jew! If a Christian do not play the knave and
get thee, I am much deceived. But adieu. These foolish
drops do somewhat drown my manly spirit. Adieu.

JESSICA
Farewell, good Launcelot.

Exit LAUNCELOT

15　Alack, what heinous sin is it in me
To be ashamed to be my father's child!
But though I am a daughter to his blood,
I am not to his manners. O Lorenzo,
If thou keep promise, I shall end this strife,
20　Become a Christian and thy loving wife.

Exit

ACT TWO, Scene 3

JESSICA and LAUNCELOT enter.

JESSICA

I'm sorry you're leaving my father like this. It's hell in our house, and you helped cheer it up, like a funny devil. But goodbye. Here's a ducat for you. You'll soon be meeting Lorenzo at supper; he'll be a guest of your new master. Give him this letter. *(gives LAUNCELOT a letter)* Do it secretly. Goodbye. I don't want my father to see me talking to you.

LAUNCELOT

Goodbye. My tears show you my feelings, my beautiful pagan, my sweet Jew! I'm sure some Christian will resort to trickery to get you. But goodbye. It's not manly to cry. Goodbye.

JESSICA

Goodbye, Launcelot.

LAUNCELOT exits.

Oh God, what a heinous sinner I am, being ashamed to be my father's child! But I need to remember I'm related to him by blood, not behavior. Oh Lorenzo, if you keep your promise to me, I'll end this agony by becoming a Christian and marrying you.

She exits.

ACT TWO, Scene 4

Enter GRATIANO, LORENZO, SALARINO, *and* SOLANIO

LORENZO
Nay, we will slink away in supper time,
Disguise us at my lodging, and return,
All in an hour.

GRATIANO
We have not made good preparation.

SALARINO
5   We have not spoke us yet of torchbearers.

SOLANIO
'Tis vile, unless it may be quaintly ordered,
And better in my mind not undertook.

LORENZO
'Tis now but four o'clock. We have two hours
To furnish us.

Enter LAUNCELOT *with a letter*

10   Friend Launcelot, what's the news?

LAUNCELOT
(giving LORENZO *the letter)*
An it shall please you to break up this, it shall seem to signify.

LORENZO
I know the hand. In faith, 'tis a fair hand,
And whiter than the paper it writ on
Is the fair hand that writ.

GRATIANO
                  Love news, in faith?

LAUNCELOT
15   *(to* LORENZO*)* By your leave, sir.

ACT TWO, Scene 4

GRATIANO, LORENZO, SALARINO, *and* SOLANIO *enter.*

LORENZO

No, we'll sneak away at supper time, disguise ourselves with masks at my house, and come back in an
hour.

GRATIANO

But we haven't made any preparations.

SALARINO

We haven't even talked about who'll be our torchbearers.

SOLANIO

The masquerade party might turn out terribly if we
don't manage things carefully. I think it's better to call
it off.

LORENZO

It's only four o'clock now. We have two hours to get
ready.

LAUNCELOT *enters with a letter.*

Launcelot, what's going on?

LAUNCELOT

(he gives LORENZO *the letter)* If you don't mind opening
this letter, you can find out for yourself.

LORENZO

I recognize the handwriting. It's beautiful handwriting. And the beautiful hand that wrote this letter is
whiter than the paper it's written on.

GRATIANO

I bet it's a love letter!

LAUNCELOT

(to LORENZO*)* May I be excused, sir?

LORENZO
Whither goest thou?

LAUNCELOT
Marry, sir, to bid my old master the Jew to sup tonight
with my new master the Christian.

LORENZO
(*giving* LAUNCELOT *money*)
Hold here, take this. Tell gentle Jessica

20   I will not fail her. Speak it privately.—
Go, gentlemen,
Will you prepare you for this masque tonight?
I am provided of a torchbearer.

Exit LAUNCELOT *the clown*

SALARINO
Ay, marry, I'll be gone about it straight.

SOLANIO
25   And so will I.

LORENZO
Meet me and Gratiano
At Gratiano's lodging some hour hence.

SALARINO
'Tis good we do so.

Exeunt SALARINO *and* SOLANIO

GRATIANO
Was not that letter from fair Jessica?

LORENZO

Where are you going?

LAUNCELOT

To invite my former boss, the Jew, to dine tonight with my new master, the Christian.

LORENZO

(he gives LAUNCELOT *money)* Hold on, take this. Tell Jessica I won't fail her. Tell her in private.—Go, gentlemen, get ready for the masquerade tonight. I have someone who can be my torchbearer.

LAUNCELOT *exits.*

SALARINO

All right, I'll go get things ready.

SOLANIO

Me too.

LORENZO

Meet me and Gratiano at his house in about an hour.

SALARINO

It's good we're doing this.

SALARINO *and* SOLANIO *exit.*

GRATIANO

Wasn't that letter from Jessica?

LORENZO

I must needs tell thee all. She hath directed

30   How I shall take her from her father's house,

What gold and jewels she is furnished with,

What page's suit she hath in readiness.

If e'er the Jew her father come to heaven,

It will be for his gentle daughter's sake.

35   And never dare Misfortune cross her foot

Unless she do it under this excuse:

That she is issue to a faithless Jew.

Come, go with me.

(gives GRATIANO *the letter)*

           Peruse this as thou goest.

Fair Jessica shall be my torchbearer.

                                 Exeunt

LORENZO

A page is a young male servant.

I have to tell you everything. She's told me how I can get her out of her father's house. She's also told me what gold and jewels she owns, and she's described the page's uniform she's keeping to wear as a disguise. If her father ever goes to heaven, it'll be because his daughter's so good. She'll never be punished with bad luck—unless it's because her father is an unbelieving Jew. Come with me. *(gives* GRATIANO *the letter)* You can look this letter over as you go. Beautiful Jessica will be my torchbearer.

They exit.

ACT TWO, Scene 5

Enter SHYLOCK *the Jew and his man* LAUNCELOT *that was the clown*

SHYLOCK
Well, thou shalt see, thy eyes shall be thy judge,
The difference of old Shylock and Bassanio.—
What, Jessica!—Thou shalt not gormandize
As thou hast done with me.—What, Jessica!—
5   And sleep and snore, and rend apparel out—
Why, Jessica, I say!

LAUNCELOT
                    Why, Jessica!

SHYLOCK
Who bids thee call? I do not bid thee call.

LAUNCELOT
Your worship was wont to tell me that I could do nothing
without bidding.

Enter JESSICA

JESSICA
10 Call you? What is your will?

SHYLOCK
I am bid forth to supper, Jessica.
There are my keys.—But wherefore should I go?
I am not bid for love. They flatter me.
But yet I'll go in hate to feed upon
15 The prodigal Christian.—Jessica, my girl,
Look to my house. I am right loath to go.
There is some ill a-brewing towards my rest,
For I did dream of money bags tonight.

ACT TWO, Scene 5

SHYLOCK *and* LAUNCELOT *enter.*

SHYLOCK

Well, you'll see it with your own eyes. You'll see the difference between working for Shylock and working for Bassanio.—*(calling for his daughter)* Jessica!—You won't eat like a pig like you used to do at my place.—Jessica!—And sleep, and snore, and wear your clothes out.—Jessica, I'm calling you!

LAUNCELOT

Jessica!

SHYLOCK

Who asked you to call her? I'm not asking you to call her.

LAUNCELOT

You always loved to tell me I couldn't do anything without being told.

JESSICA *enters.*

JESSICA

Did you call me? Do you need something?

SHYLOCK

I've been invited to supper, Jessica. Here are my keys.—But why should I go? I wasn't invited because they like me. They're just flattering me. But I'll go out of spite, to feed off the wasteful Christian.—Jessica, my girl, watch the house. I don't feel like going. Things aren't going my way right now. I know because I dreamed of money bags last night.

LAUNCELOT

20   I beseech you, sir, go. My young master doth expect your
reproach.

SHYLOCK

So do I his.

LAUNCELOT

And they have conspired together. I will not say you shall
see a masque, but if you do then it was not for nothing that
my nose fell a-bleeding on Black Monday last at six
25   o'clock i' th' morning falling out that year on Ash
Wednesday was four year in th' afternoon.

SHYLOCK

What, are there masques? Hear you me, Jessica.
Lock up my doors, and when you hear the drum
And the vile squealing of the wry-necked fife,
30   Clamber not you up to the casements then,
Nor thrust your head into the public street
To gaze on Christian fools with varnished faces.
But stop my house's ears—I mean my casements—
Let not the sound of shallow foppery enter
35   My sober house. By Jacob's staff, I swear,
I have no mind of feasting forth tonight.
But I will go.—Go you before me, sirrah.
Say I will come.

LAUNCELOT

I will go before, sir.—
Mistress, look out at window, for all this.
40   There will come a Christian by
Will be worth a Jewess' eye.

Exit **LAUNCELOT**

LAUNCELOT

> Please go, sir. My new master is expecting your approach.

SHYLOCK

> And I'm expecting his reproach.

LAUNCELOT

> And they've been plotting things together. I'm not saying you'll get a masquerade party, but if you do, I predicted it. I knew there would be a masquerade when I got that bad omen of a bloody nose last Easter Monday, at six in the morning, four years after I got the same kind of bloody nose on Ash Wednesday, in the afternoon.

SHYLOCK

> What, there's going to be a masquerade? Listen to me, Jessica, lock my doors up, and when you hear the drum and the nasty squealing of the flute, don't climb up to the windows. Don't stick your head out into the public street to stare at the Christian fools with painted faces. Block up my house's ears—I mean the windows. Don't let the noise of shallow fools enter my serious house. I swear, I'm in no mood to go out to dinner tonight, but I'll go anyway. Launcelot, go tell them I'll come.

LAUNCELOT

> I'll go ahead of you, sir. *(to JESSICA)* Mistress, be on the lookout when you're staring out the window. A Christian's coming who'll be worth a Jewess's glance.

> > > > > *LAUNCELOT exits.*

SHYLOCK
What says that fool of Hagar's offspring, ha?

JESSICA
His words were, "Farewell, mistress." Nothing else.

SHYLOCK
The patch is kind enough, but a huge feeder,
45   Snail-slow in profit, and he sleeps by day
More than the wildcat. Drones hive not with me.
Therefore I part with him, and part with him
To one that would have him help to waste
His borrowed purse. Well, Jessica, go in.
50   Perhaps I will return immediately.
Do as I bid you. Shut doors after you.
Fast bind, fast find.
A proverb never stale in thrifty mind.

Exit SHYLOCK

JESSICA
Farewell, and if my fortune be not crost,
55   I have a father, you a daughter, lost.

Exit

SHYLOCK

What did that gentile fool say to you, hmmm?

JESSICA

He said "Goodbye, madam," and nothing else.

SHYLOCK

The fool's nice enough, but he's such a huge eater, and slow as a snail when he works. He sleeps all day like a cat. Bees that don't work can't stay in my hive, so I'm letting him go, handing him off so he can waste money for his new boss, the man who borrowed money from me. Anyway, Jessica, go inside. I might come back soon. Do as I told you. Shut the doors after you. As the saying goes, lock things up, and you'll get to keep them.

He exits.

JESSICA

Goodbye. If luck's with me, I'll lose a father, and you'll lose a daughter.

She exits.

—❦—

ACT TWO, Scene 6

Enter the masquers GRATIANO *and* SALARINO

GRATIANO
This is the penthouse under which Lorenzo
Desired us to make stand.

SALARINO
His hour is almost past.

GRATIANO
And it is marvel he outdwells his hour,
For lovers ever run before the clock.

SALARINO
5   Oh, ten times faster Venus' pigeons fly
To seal love's bonds new made than they are wont
To keep obligèd faith unforfeited.

GRATIANO
That ever holds. Who riseth from a feast
With that keen appetite that he sits down?
10   Where is the horse that doth untread again
His tedious measures with the unbated fire
That he did pace them first? All things that are,
Are with more spirit chasèd than enjoyed. How
like a younker or a prodigal
15   The scarfèd bark puts from her native bay,
Hugged and embraèd by the strumpet wind!
How like the prodigal doth she return,
With overweathered ribs and ragged sails
Lean, rent, and beggared by the strumpet wind!

SALARINO
20   Here comes Lorenzo. More of this hereafter.

Enter LORENZO

ACT TWO, Scene 6

GRATIANO *and* SALARINO *enter, dressed for the masquerade ball.*

GRATIANO

This is the roof under which Lorenzo said to meet him.

SALARINO

He's late.

GRATIANO

Yes, and that's surprising, because lovers are usually early.

SALARINO

Yes, for new lovers time passes ten times faster than for couples who've been married forever.

GRATIANO

That's always true. Who gets up from a meal with the same appetite he had when he sat down? Can any horse retrace his footsteps with the same energy he had when he walked them the first time? We chase everything in life more excitedly than we actually enjoy it when we get it. It's like when a ship sails out of the harbor with all its flags waving, gently pushed by the wind. When that ship returns, her timber is all weather-beaten and her sails are ragged. That same wind makes the ship thin and poor.

SALARINO

Here comes Lorenzo. We'll talk about this later.

LORENZO *enters.*

LORENZO
Sweet friends, your patience for my long abode.
Not I but my affairs have made you wait.
When you shall please to play the thieves for wives,
I'll watch as long for you then. Approach.
25   Here dwells my father Jew.—Ho! Who's within?

Enter JESSICA *above, disguised as a boy*

JESSICA
Who are you? Tell me for more certainty,
Albeit I'll swear that I do know your tongue.

LORENZO
Lorenzo, and thy love.

JESSICA
Lorenzo certain, and my love indeed—
30   For who love I so much? And now who knows
But you, Lorenzo, whether I am yours?

LORENZO
Heaven and thy thoughts are witness that thou art.

JESSICA
Here, catch this casket. It is worth the pains.
I am glad 'tis night, you do not look on me,
35   For I am much ashamed of my exchange.
But love is blind, and lovers cannot see
The pretty follies that themselves commit,
For if they could Cupid himself would blush
To see me thus transformèd to a boy.

LORENZO
40   Descend, for you must be my torchbearer.

JESSICA
What, must I hold a candle to my shames?
They in themselves, good sooth, are too too light.
Why, 'tis an office of discovery, love.
And I should be obscured.

LORENZO

My dear friends, thanks for your patience. I had business that made me late. When you have to steal your own wives some day, I'll wait for you just as long. Come over here. My future father-in-law, the Jew, lives here.—Hey! Who's in there?

JESSICA *appears above, disguised as a boy.*

JESSICA

Who are you? Tell me so I can be sure, though I swear I recognize your voice.

LORENZO

I'm Lorenzo, your love.

JESSICA

Lorenzo, that's for sure, and I'm also sure you're my love—who else do I love so much? And now who but you knows whether I'm yours?

LORENZO

As God is my witness, you know you're mine.

JESSICA

Here, catch this box. It'll be worth your while. I'm glad it's nighttime and you can't see me. I'm ashamed of my disguise. But love is blind, and lovers can't see the silly things they do around each other. If they could, Cupid himself would be embarassed to see me dressed up as a boy.

LORENZO

Come down here. You have to be my torchbearer for the masquerade.

JESSICA

What, I have to hold a candle up so people can see what I'm doing? The truth is, I'm behaving like a loose woman. The torchbearer is supposed to bring light and love, but I should be hidden away in the dark.

LORENZO

So are you, sweet,

45   Even in the lovely garnish of a boy.

But come at once,

For the close night doth play the runaway,

And we are stayed for at Bassanio's feast.

JESSICA

I will make fast the doors and gild myself

50   With some more ducats, and be with you straight.

Exit JESSICA *above*

GRATIANO

Now, by my hood, a gentile and no Jew.

LORENZO

Beshrew me but I love her heartily.

For she is wise, if I can judge of her.

And fair she is, if that mine eyes be true.

55   And true she is, as she hath proved herself.

And therefore, like herself—wise, fair and true—

Shall she be placèd in my constant soul.

Enter JESSICA

What, art thou come?—On, gentlemen, away!

Our masquing mates by this time for us stay.

Exit LORENZO *with* JESSICA *and* SALARINO

Enter ANTONIO

ANTONIO

60   Who's there?

GRATIANO

Signor Antonio?

LORENZO

You're hidden away, sweetheart, dressed up like a boy. Come on quickly. Time flies at night, and we're late for Bassanio's feast.

JESSICA

I'll lock up the doors, grab some more ducats, and be with you right away.

JESSICA exits from above.

GRATIANO

My God, she can't be a Jew, she's too nice!

LORENZO

God, I'm crazy about her. She's wise, if I'm judging her right. She's beautiful, if my eyes can see. And she's loyal, as she has proven. And as long as she's herself—wise, beautiful, and faithful—she'll always have a place in my heart.

JESSICA enters.

Ah, you're here?—Come on, gentlemen, let's go! Our masquerade mates are waiting for us.

LORENZO, JESSICA, and SALARINO exit.

ANTONIO enters.

ANTONIO

Who's there?

GRATIANO

Signor Antonio?

ANTONIO
Fie, fie, Gratiano! Where are all the rest?
'Tis nine o'clock. Our friends all stay for you.
No masque tonight. The wind is come about.
Bassanio presently will go aboard.
65   I have sent twenty out to seek for you.

GRATIANO
I am glad on 't. I desire no more delight
Than to be under sail and gone tonight.

Exeunt

ANTONIO

Gratiano, where is everybody? It's nine o'clock! Our friends are all waiting for you. There's no masquerade tonight. The wind is blowing right, so Bassanio's going onboard immediately. I've sent twenty people to look for you.

GRATIANO

I'm glad. I want to head out tonight.

They exit.

ACT TWO, Scene 7

Flourish cornets
Enter PORTIA *with the Prince of* MOROCCO, *and both their*
trains

PORTIA
(to servant) Go draw aside the curtains and discover
The several caskets to this noble prince.—

A curtain is drawn showing a gold, silver, and lead casket

(to MOROCCO*)* Now make your choice.

MOROCCO
5   The first, of gold, who this inscription bears:
"Who chooseth me shall gain what many men desire."
The second, silver, which this promise carries:
"Who chooseth me shall get as much as he deserves."
This third, dull lead, with warning all as blunt:
10   "Who chooseth me must give and hazard all he hath."
How shall I know if I do choose the right?

PORTIA
The one of them contains my picture, Prince.
If you choose that, then I am yours withal.

MOROCCO
Some god direct my judgment! Let me see.
15   I will survey th' inscriptions back again.
What says this leaden casket?
"Who chooseth me must give and hazard all he hath."
Must give—for what? For lead? Hazard for lead?
This casket threatens. Men that hazard all
20   Do it in hope of fair advantages.
A golden mind stoops not to shows of dross.
I'll then nor give nor hazard aught for lead.
What says the silver with her virgin hue?

ACT TWO, Scene 7

Trumpets play. PORTIA *enters with the prince of* MOROCCO *and both their entourages.*

PORTIA

(to servant) Go open the curtains and show the different boxes to the prince.

A curtain is drawn revealing three caskets: one gold, one silver, and one lead.

(to MOROCCO*)* Now make your choice.

MOROCCO

The first one, the gold one, has an inscription that says, "He who chooses me will get what many men want." The second one, the silver one, says, "He who chooses me will get what he deserves." And this third one is made of dull lead. It has a blunt warning that says, "He who chooses me must give and risk all he has." How will I know if I chose the right one?

PORTIA

One of them contains my picture. If you choose that one, I'm yours, along with the picture.

MOROCCO

I wish some god could help me choose! Let me see. I'll look over the inscriptions again. What does the lead box say? "He who chooses me must give and risk all he has." Must give everything—for what? For lead? Risk everything for lead? This box is too threatening. Men who risk everything hope to make profits. A golden mind doesn't bend down to choose something worthless. So I won't give or risk anything for lead. What does the silver one say?

"Who chooseth me shall get as much as he deserves."

25 "As much as he deserves!"—pause there, Morocco,
And weigh thy value with an even hand.
If thou beest rated by thy estimation,
Thou dost deserve enough, and yet enough
May not extend so far as to the lady,

30 And yet to be afeard of my deserving
Were but a weak disabling of myself.
As much as I deserve! Why, that's the lady.
I do in birth deserve her, and in fortunes,
In graces, and in qualities of breeding.

35 But more than these, in love I do deserve.
What if I strayed no further, but chose here?
Let's see once more this saying graved in gold,
"Who chooseth me shall gain what many men desire."
Why, that's the lady. All the world desires her.

40 From the four corners of the earth they come
To kiss this shrine, this mortal breathing saint.
The Hyrcanian deserts and the vasty wilds
Of wide Arabia are as thoroughfares now
For princes to come view fair Portia.

45 The watery kingdom, whose ambitious head
Spits in the face of heaven, is no bar
To stop the foreign spirits, but they come
As o'er a brook to see fair Portia.
One of these three contains her heavenly picture.

50 Is 't like that lead contains her? 'Twere damnation
To think so base a thought. It were too gross
To rib her cerecloth in the obscure grave.
Or shall I think in silver she's immured,
Being ten times undervalued to tried gold?

55 O sinful thought! Never so rich a gem
Was set in worse than gold. They have in England
A coin that bears the figure of an angel
Stamped in gold, but that's insculped upon.
But here an angel in a golden bed

"He who chooses me will get as much as he deserves." As much as he deserves—wait a minute there, Morocco, and consider your own value with a level head. If your reputation is trustworthy, you deserve a lot—though maybe not enough to include this lady. But fearing I don't deserve her is a way of underestimating myself. As much as I deserve—I deserve Portia! By birth I deserve her. In terms of wealth, talents, and upbringing, and especially love, I deserve her. What if I went no further and chose this one? But let's see once more what the gold one says: "He who chooses me will get what many men want." That's Portia! The whole world wants her. They come from the four corners of the earth to kiss this shrine and see this living, breathing saint. Princes travel across deserts and the vast wilderness of Arabia to come see the beautiful Portia. The wide ocean doesn't prevent them from coming to see her—they travel across it as if it were a little stream. One of these three boxes contains her lovely picture. Could the lead one contain it? No, it'd be a sin to think such a low thought. Lead's too crass to hold her. Is she enclosed in silver, which is ten times less valuable than gold? Oh, what a sinful thought! Nobody ever set a gem like her in a worse setting than gold. They have a coin in England stamped with the figure of an angel, but that's just engraved on the surface.

60 Lies all within.—Deliver me the key.
Here do I choose, and thrive I as I may!

PORTIA
(*giving* MOROCCO *a key*)
There, take it, Prince. And if my form lie there
Then I am yours.

MOROCCO *opens the golden casket*

MOROCCO
O hell, what have we here?
65 A carrion death, within whose empty eye
There is a written scroll. I'll read the writing.
(*reads*)
"All that glisters is not gold—
Often have you heard that told.
Many a man his life hath sold
70 But my outside to behold.
Gilded tombs do worms enfold.
Had you been as wise as bold,
Young in limbs, in judgment old,
Your answer had not been inscrolled.
75 Fare you well. Your suit is cold—
Cold, indeed, and labor lost."
Then, farewell, heat, and welcome, frost!
Portia, adieu. I have too grieved a heart
To take a tedious leave. Thus losers part.

Exit MOROCCO *with his train*

PORTIA
80 A gentle riddance.—Draw the curtains, go.—
Let all of his complexion choose me so.

Exeunt

Here an angel's lying in a golden bed.—Give me the key. I will choose this one and try my chances.

PORTIA

(she hands him a key) There, take it, prince. And if my picture's in there, then I'm yours.

MOROCCO *opens the gold casket.*

MOROCCO

Damn it! What's this? It's a skull with a scroll in its empty eye socket. I'll read it aloud.
(he reads)
"All that glitters is not gold—
You've often heard that said.
Many men have sold their souls
Just to view my shiny surface.
But gilded tombs contain worms.
If you'd been as wise as you were bold,
With an old man's mature judgment,
You wouldn't have had to read this scroll.
So goodbye—you lost your chance."
Lost my chance indeed! So goodbye hope, and hello despair. Portia, goodbye to you. My heart's too sad for long goodbyes. Losers always leave quickly.

MOROCCO *exits with his entourage.*

PORTIA

Good riddance!—Close the curtains and leave.—I hope everyone who looks like him will make the same choice.

They exit.

ACT TWO, Scene 8

Enter SALARINO *and* SOLANIO

SALARINO
Why, man, I saw Bassanio under sail.
With him is Gratiano gone along.
And in their ship I am sure Lorenzo is not.

SOLANIO
The villain Jew with outcries raised the Duke,
5　Who went with him to search Bassanio's ship.

SALARINO
He came too late. The ship was under sail.
But there the Duke was given to understand
That in a gondola were seen together
Lorenzo and his amorous Jessica.
10　Besides, Antonio certified the Duke
They were not with Bassanio in his ship.

SOLANIO
I never heard a passion so confused,
So strange, outrageous, and so variable,
As the dog Jew did utter in the streets.
15　"My daughter! O my ducats! O my daughter,
Fled with a Christian! O my Christian ducats!
Justice, the law, my ducats, and my daughter!
A sealèd bag, two sealèd bags of ducats,
Of double ducats, stol'n from me by my daughter!
20　And jewels—two stones, two rich and precious stones—
Stol'n by my daughter! Justice, find the girl!
She hath the stones upon her, and the ducats."

SALARINO
Why, all the boys in Venice follow him,
Crying, "His stones, his daughter, and his ducats!"

ACT TWO, Scene 8

SALARINO *and* SOLANIO *enter.*

SALARINO

I saw Bassanio sail away, and Gratiano went with him. I'm sure Lorenzo isn't on their ship.

SOLANIO

That wicked Jew got the duke to listen to his complaints. The duke went with him to search Bassanio's ship.

SALARINO

He got there too late. The ship was already sailing. But once he got there, the duke learned that Lorenzo and his lover Jessica were together in a gondola. In any case, Antonio assured the duke they weren't with Bassanio on his ship.

SOLANIO

I've never heard such confused emotions as what that Jew dog was shouting in the streets. "My daughter, oh my ducats, oh my daughter! Ran off with a Christian! Oh my Christian ducats! Justice, the law, my ducats, and my daughter, a sealed bag, two sealed bags of ducats, of double ducats, stolen from me by my daughter, and jewels—two stones, two rich and precious stones—stolen by my daughter! Justice, find the girl! She has the stones on her, and the ducats."

SALARINO

I know, all the boys in Venice are following him, yelling, "His stones, his daughter, and his ducats!"

SOLANIO

25   Let good Antonio look he keep his day,
        Or he shall pay for this.

SALARINO

                              Marry, well remembered.
        I reasoned with a Frenchman yesterday,
        Who told me, in the narrow seas that part
        The French and English, there miscarried
30   A vessel of our country richly fraught.
        I thought upon Antonio when he told me,
        And wished in silence that it were not his.

SOLANIO

        You were best to tell Antonio what you hear—
        Yet do not suddenly, for it may grieve him.

SALARINO

35   A kinder gentleman treads not the earth.
        I saw Bassanio and Antonio part.
        Bassanio told him he would make some speed
        Of his return. He answered, "Do not so.
        Slubber not business for my sake, Bassanio
40   But stay the very riping of the time.
        And for the Jew's bond which he hath of me,
        Let it not enter in your mind of love.
        Be merry, and employ your chiefest thoughts
        To courtship and such fair ostents of love
45   As shall conveniently become you there."
        And even there, his eye being big with tears,
        Turning his face, he put his hand behind him,
        And with affection wondrous sensible
        He wrung Bassanio's hand. And so they parted.

SOLANIO

I hope Antonio repays his loan on time, or he'll suffer for this.

SALARINO

That's a good point. I spoke with a Frenchman yesterday who said that a Venetian ship loaded with treasure was wrecked in the English Channel. I thought about Antonio when he told me. I silently hoped it wasn't his ship.

SOLANIO

You should tell Antonio what you hear—but don't do it suddenly, because it might upset him.

SALARINO

There's no nicer guy in the whole world. I saw Bassanio and Antonio say goodbye. Bassanio told him he'd try to hurry back. Antonio answered "Don't rush. Don't do a sloppy job for my sake, Bassanio. Stay until everything is finished. As for the Jew's contract, don't let it be a factor in your plans. Be happy and concentrate your thoughts on love and how to win your love." Then his eyes started tearing up. He turned his face away. Then he shook Bassanio's hand affectionately—and they separated.

SOLANIO

50   I think he only loves the world for him.
        I pray thee, let us go and find him out
        And quicken his embracèd heaviness
        With some delight or other.

SALARINO

                                    Do we so.

                                            Exeunt

SOLANIO

I think he only loves life because of Bassanio. Let's go find him and cheer him up.

SALARINO

Yes, let's do that.

They exit.

ACT TWO, Scene 9

Enter NERISSA *and a servitor*

NERISSA
Quick, quick, I pray thee. Draw the curtain straight.
The Prince of Arragon hath ta'en his oath
And comes to his election presently.

Flourish cornets
Enter the Prince of ARRAGON, *his train, and* PORTIA

PORTIA
Behold, there stand the caskets, noble Prince.
5   If you choose that wherein I am contained,
Straight shall our nuptial rites be solemnized.
But if you fail, without more speech, my lord,
You must be gone from hence immediately.

ARRAGON
I am enjoined by oath to observe three things:
10   First, never to unfold to any one
Which casket 'twas I chose; next, if I fail
Of the right casket, never in my life
To woo a maid in way of marriage; lastly,
If I do fail in fortune of my choice,
15   Immediately to leave you and be gone.

PORTIA
To these injunctions every one doth swear
That comes to hazard for my worthless self.

ARRAGON
And so have I addressed me. Fortune now
To my heart's hope! Gold, silver, and base lead.
20   "Who chooseth me must give and hazard all he hath."
You shall look fairer ere I give or hazard.
What says the golden chest? Ha, let me see.
"Who chooseth me shall gain what many men desire."

ACT TWO, Scene 9

NERISSA *and a servant enter.*

NERISSA

Hurry, hurry, close the curtain quick. The prince of Arragon has taken his oath, and he's coming to make his choice now.

Trumpets play. The Prince of ARRAGON, his entourage, and PORTIA enter.

PORTIA

Look, here are the boxes, prince. If you choose the one that contains my picture, we'll be married right away. But if you fail, you have to leave immediately. No pleas will be allowed.

ARRAGON

I swore I'd do three things. First, I can never tell anyone what box I choose. Second, if I choose the wrong box, I'll never propose marriage for the rest of my life. Third, if I pick the wrong box, I'll leave immediately.

PORTIA

Everyone who comes to gamble on winning me has to swear to these three rules.

ARRAGON

Okay, I'm ready. I hope luck will give me what my heart hopes for! Gold, silver, and common lead. "He who chooses me must give and risk all he has." You'd have to be more attractive for me to give or risk anything for you. What does the golden box say? Hmm, let me see:

"What many men desire"—that "many" may be meant
25   By the fool multitude that choose by show,
Not learning more than the fond eye doth teach;
Which pries not to th' interior, but like the martlet
Builds in the weather on the outward wall,
Even in the force and road of casualty.
30   I will not choose what many men desire
Because I will not jump with common spirits
And rank me with the barbarous multitudes.
Why then, to thee, thou silver treasure house.
Tell me once more what title thou dost bear.
35   "Who chooseth me shall get as much as he deserves."
And well said too—for who shall go about
To cozen fortune and be honorable
Without the stamp of merit? Let none presume
To wear an undeservèd dignity.
40   Oh, that estates, degrees and offices
Were not derived corruptly, and that clear honor
Were purchased by the merit of the wearer!
How many then should cover that stand bare!
How many be commanded that command!
45   How much low peasantry would then be gleaned
From the true seed of honor! And how much honor
Picked from the chaff and ruin of the times
To be new varnished! Well, but to my choice.
"Who chooseth me shall get as much as he deserves."
50   I will assume desert.—Give me a key for this,
And instantly unlock my fortunes here.

ARRAGON *opens the silver casket*

PORTIA
Too long a pause for that which you find there.

"He who chooses me will get what many men want." What many men want—that "many" could mean that most people are fools and choose by whatever is flashy. They don't go beyond what their eyes see. They don't bother to find out what's on the inside. Just like those birds called martins who build their nests on the outside of walls, people pay too much attention to what's on the outside. So I won't choose what many men desire, because I won't jump on the bandwagon and include myself with the whole crude population. So I guess it's you, you silver treasure house. Tell me once more what you say. "He who chooses me will get what he deserves." That's nicely put—because who's going to cheat luck and get more than he deserves? No one should have an honor he doesn't deserve. Oh, wouldn't it be great if property, rank, official positions, and other honors were earned only by merit, not by corruption? There wouldn't be too many important men then. How many people who are humble now would be great then? How many people who give orders now would have to take orders? How many noblemen would be weeded out and would become peasants? And how many common people would suddenly shine with nobility? Well, let me get back to my choice. "He who chooses me will get what he deserves." I'll assume I deserve the very best.—Give me a key for this one. I'll unlock my fate here in a second.

ARRAGON *opens the silver casket.*

PORTIA

You thought about it too long, considering what you found there.

ARRAGON

What's here? The portrait of a blinking idiot
Presenting me a schedule! I will read it.—

55 How much unlike art thou to Portia!
How much unlike my hopes and my deservings!
"Who chooseth me shall have as much as he deserves"!
Did I deserve no more than a fool's head?
Is that my prize? Are my deserts no better?

PORTIA

60 To offend and judge are distinct offices
And of opposèd natures.

ARRAGON

What is here?

(reads)

"The fire seven times tried this,
Seven times tried that judgment is,
That did never choose amiss.

65 Some there be that shadows kiss.
Such have but a shadow's bliss.
There be fools alive, iwis,
Silvered o'er—and so was this.
Take what wife you will to bed,

70 I will ever be your head.
So be gone. You are sped."

Still more fool I shall appear
By the time I linger here.
With one fool's head I came to woo,

75 But I go away with two.—
Sweet, adieu. I'll keep my oath
Patiently to bear my wroth."

Exeunt ARRAGON *and his train*

ARRAGON

What's this? A picture of an idiot holding a scroll up for me to read! I'll read it.—It looks so unlike Portia! This outcome isn't what I hoped for, or what I deserve. "The one who chooses me will get what he deserves"! Didn't I deserve anything more than a fool's head? Is this my prize? Don't I deserve more than this?

PORTIA

Judging what you deserve is one thing. Offending you is something very different, so I'll keep my mouth shut.

ARRAGON

What does this say?
(he reads)

> "This box was tested in the fire seven times.
> The person who never makes a wrong choice
> Has wisdom that will stand the test.
> Some people kiss shadows.
> They only feel the shadow of joy.
> There are fools out there
> With silver hair and silver coins.
> This choice was as foolish as they are.
> Take whatever wife you want to bed with you,
> You'll have a fool's head forever.
> So go away. You're done here."

The longer I stay, the more foolish I look. I came here with a fool's head on my shoulders and now I'm leaving with two.—Goodbye, sweet lady. I'll keep my oath and patiently suffer through my anger.

He exits with his train.

ACT TWO

PORTIA
Thus hath the candle singed the moth.
O these deliberate fools! When they do choose,
80   They have the wisdom by their wit to lose.

NERISSA
The ancient saying is no heresy.
Hanging and wiving goes by destiny.

PORTIA
Come, draw the curtain, Nerissa.

Enter MESSENGER

MESSENGER
85   Where is my lady?

PORTIA
                              Here. What would my lord?

MESSENGER
Madam, there is alighted at your gate
A young Venetian, one that comes before
To signify th' approaching of his lord,
From whom he bringeth sensible regreets,
90   To wit—besides commends and courteous breath—
Gifts of rich value. Yet I have not seen
So likely an ambassador of love.
A day in April never came so sweet
To show how costly summer was at hand,
95   As this forespurrer comes before his lord.

PORTIA
No more, I pray thee. I am half afeard
Thou wilt say anon he is some kin to thee,
Thou spend'st such high-day wit in praising him.—
Come, come, Nerissa, for I long to see
100 Quick Cupid's post that comes so mannerly.

NERISSA
Bassanio, Lord Love, if thy will it be!

Exeunt

PORTIA

These men are like moths, drawn to these boxes as if they were flames. This is how the candle burned the moth. Oh, these fools! When they choose, they only know how to lose.

NERISSA

You know what they say. Destiny chooses when you'll die and who you'll marry.

PORTIA

Come on, close the curtain, Nerissa.

A **MESSENGER** *enters.*

MESSENGER

Where's lady Portia?

PORTIA

Here. How can I help you, sir?

MESSENGER

Madam, a young Venetian man has arrived to tell us his master is about to arrive. This lord has sent gifts. Besides his nice polite greetings, his gifts are expensive. I haven't seen such a promising candidate for your love. This servant has arrived before his master the way a sweet spring day hints about a lush summer. But there's never been an April day as promising as this.

PORTIA

Please don't tell me any more. I'm almost afraid you're going to tell me he's a relative of yours, because you're going so crazy praising him. Come on, Nerissa, I want to go see this man who's come so courteously.

NERISSA

I hope it's Bassanio coming to win Portia!

They exit.

ACT THREE

Scene 1

Enter SOLANIO *and* SALARINO

SOLANIO
Now, what news on the Rialto?

SALARINO
Why, yet it lives there unchecked that Antonio hath a
ship of rich lading wrecked on the narrow seas. The
Goodwins I think they call the place—a very dangerous
5   flat, and fatal, where the carcasses of many a tall ship lie
buried, as they say, if my gossip report be an honest
woman of her word.

SOLANIO
I would she were as lying a gossip in that as ever knapped
ginger or made her neighbors believe she wept for the
10   death of a third husband. But it is true, without any slips
of prolixity or crossing the plain highway of talk, that the
good Antonio, the honest Antonio—oh, that I had a title
good enough to keep his name company!—

SALARINO
Come, the full stop.

SOLANIO
15   Ha, what sayest thou? Why, the end is he hath lost a ship.

SALARINO
I would it might prove the end of his losses.

SOLANIO
Let me say "Amen" betimes, lest the devil cross my
prayer, for here he comes in the likeness of a Jew.

Enter SHYLOCK

ACT THREE

Scene 1

SOLANIO *and* SALARINO *enter.*

SOLANIO
So, what's the news on the Rialto?

SALARINO
Well, there's a rumor that Antonio had a ship carrying expensive cargo that shipwrecked in the English Channel on the Goodwin Sands, a very dangerous sandbar. Many ships have sunk there, according to rumors.

SOLANIO
I hope this new rumor is a lie, like the gossiping widow's claim that she was sorry her third husband died! But it's true—I don't want to get all mushy and go on and on, but the good Antonio, the honest Antonio—oh, if I only had a title good enough to match his!—

SALARINO
Come on, get to the point.

SOLANIO
What are you saying? Well, the point is, he's lost a ship.

SALARINO
I hope that's all he loses.

SOLANIO
Let me say "amen" quickly, before the devil comes in and stops my prayer—because here comes the devil, disguised as a Jew.

SHYLOCK *enters.*

How now, Shylock? What news among the merchants?

SHYLOCK

20   You knew—none so well, none so well as you—of my
daughter's flight.

SALARINO

That's certain. I, for my part, knew the tailor that made
the wings she flew withal.

SOLANIO

And Shylock, for his own part, knew the bird was fledged,
25   and then it is the complexion of them all to leave the dam.

SHYLOCK

She is damned for it.

SOLANIO

That's certain—if the devil may be her judge.

SHYLOCK

My own flesh and blood to rebel!

SOLANIO

Out upon it, old carrion! Rebels it at these years?

SHYLOCK

30   I say my daughter is my flesh and blood.

SALARINO

There is more difference between thy flesh and hers than
between jet and ivory, more between your bloods than
there is between red wine and rhenish. But tell us, do you
hear whether Antonio have had any loss at sea or no?

How's it going, Shylock? What's the news among the merchants?

SHYLOCK

You knew—no one knew, no one knew as well as you did—about my daughter's plans to run away.

SALARINO

That's true. I even knew the tailor who made the disguise she wore when she ran off.

SOLANIO

And Shylock knew his daughter was ready to run away. It's natural for children to leave their parents.

SHYLOCK

She'll be damned for it.

SALARINO

That's true—if the devil's judging her.

SHYLOCK

My own flesh and blood turned against me! A rebel!

SOLANIO

No! Your flesh still rebels at your age?

Solanio pretends to think Shylock means he can't control his own sexual urges.

SHYLOCK

I mean my daughter is my flesh and blood.

SALARINO

You two are totally different. Your flesh is more different from hers than coal is from ivory. There's more difference between your bloods than between red wine and white. But tell us, did you hear anything about Antonio's loss at sea?

SHYLOCK

35   There I have another bad match!—a bankrupt, a prodigal
who dare scarce show his head on the Rialto, a beggar that
was used to come so smug upon the mart. Let him look to
his bond. He was wont to call me usurer; let him look to
his bond. He was wont to lend money for a Christian
40   courtesy; let him look to his bond.

SALARINO

Why, I am sure, if he forfeit thou wilt not take his flesh.
What's that good for?

SHYLOCK

To bait fish withal. If it will feed nothing else, it will feed
my revenge. He hath disgraced me and hindered me half
45   a million, laughed at my losses, mocked at my gains,
scorned my nation, thwarted my bargains, cooled my
friends, heated mine enemies—and what's his reason? I
am a Jew. Hath not a Jew eyes? Hath not a Jew hands,
organs, dimensions, senses, affections, passions? Fed
50   with the same food, hurt with the same weapons, subject
to the same diseases, healed by the same means, warmed
and cooled by the same winter and summer as a Christian
is? If you prick us, do we not bleed? If you tickle us, do we
not laugh? If you poison us, do we not die? And if you
55   wrong us, shall we not revenge? If we are like you in the
rest, we will resemble you in that. If a Jew wrong a
Christian, what is his humility? Revenge. If a Christian
wrong a Jew, what should his sufferance be by Christian
example? Why, revenge. The villainy you teach me I will
60   execute—and it shall go hard but I will better the
instruction.

SHYLOCK

That's another bad deal I've made!—a bankrupt, a spendthrift, who now has to hide his head on the Rialto, a beggar who used to look so smug in front of the other merchants. Let him think about his own debt. He liked to call me a loan shark; let him think about his debt to me. He used to lend money as a favor between Christians; but now, let him think about his own debt.

SALARINO

But you won't take his flesh if he can't pay. What's that good for?

SHYLOCK

I'll use it for fish bait. You can't eat human flesh, but if it feeds nothing else, it'll feed my revenge. He's insulted me and cost me half a million ducats. He's laughed at my losses, made fun of my earnings, humiliated my race, thwarted my deals, turned my friends against me, riled up my enemies—and why? Because I'm a Jew. Doesn't a Jew have eyes? Doesn't a Jew have hands, bodily organs, a human shape, five senses, feelings, and passions? Doesn't a Jew eat the same food, get hurt with the same weapons, get sick with the same diseases, get healed by the same medicine, and warm up in summer and cool off in winter just like a Christian? If you prick us with a pin, don't we bleed? If you tickle us, don't we laugh? If you poison us, don't we die? And if you treat us badly, won't we try to get revenge? If we're like you in everything else, we'll resemble you in that respect. If a Jew offends a Christian, what's the Christian's kind and gentle reaction? Revenge. If a Christian offends a Jew, what punishment will he come up with if he follows the Christian example? Of course, the same thing—revenge! I'll treat you as badly as you Christians taught me to— and you'll be lucky if I don't outdo my teachers.

Enter a MAN *from* ANTONIO

MAN
(to SOLANIO *and* SALARINO*)* Gentlemen, my master
Antonio is at his house and desires to speak with you
both.

SALARINO
65   We have been up and down to seek him.

Enter TUBAL

SOLANIO
Here comes another of the tribe. A third cannot be
matched unless the devil himself turn Jew.

Exeunt SOLANIO, SALARINO, *and* MAN

SHYLOCK
How now, Tubal? What news from Genoa? Hast thou
found my daughter?

TUBAL
70   I often came where I did hear of her, but cannot find her.

SHYLOCK
Why, there, there, there, there! A diamond gone cost me
two thousand ducats in Frankfurt—the curse never fell
upon our nation till now! I never felt it till now—Two
thousand ducats in that, and other precious, precious
75   jewels. I would my daughter were dead at my foot and the
jewels in her ear! Would she were hearsed at my foot and
the ducats in her coffin! No news of them? Why, so. And
I know not what's spent in the search. Why thou, loss
upon loss! The thief gone with so much, and so much to
80   find the thief—and no satisfaction, no revenge. Nor no ill
luck stirring but what lights o' my shoulders, no sighs but
o' my breathing, no tears but o' my shedding.

One of ANTONIO'S SERVANTS *enters.*

SERVANT

(to SOLANIO *and* SALARINO*)* My master Antonio is at his house and would like to speak to you both.

SALARINO

We've been looking for him everywhere.

TUBAL *enters.*

SOLANIO

Here comes another Jew. You couldn't find a third like these two unless the devil himself turned into a Jew.

SOLANIO, SALARINO, *and* ANTONIO'S SERVANT *exit.*

SHYLOCK

Hello, Tubal. Any news from Genoa? Did you find my daughter?

TUBAL

I went to many places where I heard news about her, but I couldn't find her.

SHYLOCK

Oh, oh, oh! One of the stolen diamonds cost me two thousand ducats in Frankfurt! I never felt the curse of the Jews until now. I never felt it until now—two thousand ducats in that diamond, and other precious, precious jewels! I wish my daughter were dead at my feet wearing those jewels! I wish she were in her coffin here, with the ducats in her coffin! You couldn't find out anything about them? Why? I don't even know how much I'm spending to find them. Loss upon loss! The thief left with so much, and I'm spending so much to hunt down the thief—and still I'm not satisfied! I haven't gotten my revenge. The only luck I have is bad luck. Nobody suffers but me. Nobody's crying except me.

TUBAL

Yes, other men have ill luck too. Antonio, as I heard in
Genoa—

SHYLOCK

85   What, what, what? Ill luck, ill luck?

TUBAL

Hath an argosy cast away coming from Tripolis.

SHYLOCK

I thank God, I thank God! Is 't true, is 't true?

TUBAL

I spoke with some of the sailors that escaped the wreck.

SHYLOCK

I thank thee, good Tubal. Good news, good news! Ha, ha,
90   heard in Genoa.

TUBAL

Your daughter spent in Genoa, as I heard, in one night
fourscore ducats.

SHYLOCK

Thou stickest a dagger in me. I shall never see my gold
again. Fourscore ducats at a sitting! Fourscore ducats!

TUBAL

95   There came divers of Antonio's creditors in my company
to Venice that swear he cannot choose but break.

SHYLOCK

I am very glad of it. I'll plague him. I'll torture him. I am
glad of it.

TUBAL

One of them showed me a ring that he had of your
100   daughter for a monkey.

SHYLOCK

Out upon her! Thou torturest me, Tubal. It was my
turquoise. I had it of Leah when I was a bachelor. I would
not have given it for a wilderness of monkeys.

TUBAL

Well, other men have bad luck too. Antonio, as I heard in Genoa—

SHYLOCK

What, what, what? Bad luck, bad luck?

TUBAL

He's had a ship wrecked coming from Tripolis.

SHYLOCK

Thank God, thank God! Is it true, is it true?

TUBAL

I spoke with some of the sailors who survived the wreck.

SHYLOCK

Thank you, Tubal. Good news, good news! Ha, ha, heard in Genoa.

TUBAL

I also heard that your daughter spent eighty ducats in Genoa one night.

SHYLOCK

Oh, you're sticking a dagger in me! I'll never see my gold again. Eighty ducats in one shot! Eighty ducats!

TUBAL

I came to Venice with a number of Antonio's creditors who say he won't be able to avoid going bankrupt.

SHYLOCK

I'm very glad about that. I'll hound him. I'll torture him. I'm very glad.

TUBAL

One creditor showed me a ring he got from your daughter in exchange for a monkey.

SHYLOCK

Damn her! You're torturing me, Tubal. That was my turquoise ring! Leah gave it to me before we were married. I wouldn't have given it away for a whole jungle of monkeys.

TUBAL
But Antonio is certainly undone.

SHYLOCK
105 Nay, that's true, that's very true. Go, Tubal, fee me an officer. Bespeak him a fortnight before.—I will have the heart of him if he forfeit, for were he out of Venice I can make what merchandise I will.—Go, go, Tubal, and meet me at our synagogue. Go, good Tubal. At our synagogue,
110 Tubal.

Exeunt severally

TUBAL

But Antonio's certainly ruined.

SHYLOCK

That's true, that's very true. Tubal, go find me a police officer to arrest Antonio. Get him ready two weeks ahead of time.—I'll take Antonio's heart if he can't pay. With him out of Venice, I can make whatever bargains I want when I lend money.—Go, Tubal. Meet me at the synagogue.

They exit.

ACT THREE, Scene 2

Enter BASSANIO, PORTIA, GRATIANO, NERISSA, *and all their trains, including a* SINGER

PORTIA
(to BASSANIO*)* I pray you, tarry. Pause a day or two
Before you hazard, for in choosing wrong
I lose your company. Therefore forbear awhile.
There's something tells me—but it is not love—
5   I would not lose you, and you know yourself
Hate counsels not in such a quality.
But lest you should not understand me well—
And yet a maiden hath no tongue but thought—
I would detain you here some month or two
10   Before you venture for me. I could teach you
How to choose right, but I am then forsworn.
So will I never be. So may you miss me.
But if you do, you'll make me wish a sin,
That I had been forsworn. Beshrew your eyes,
15   They have o'erlooked me and divided me.
One half of me is yours, the other half yours—
Mine own, I would say. But if mine, then yours,
And so all yours. Oh, these naughty times
Put bars between the owners and their rights!
20   And so, though yours, not yours. Prove it so.
Let Fortune go to hell for it, not I.
I speak too long, but 'tis to peize the time,
To eke it and to draw it out in length,
To stay you from election.

BASSANIO
                                Let me choose,
25   For as I am, I live upon the rack.

PORTIA
Upon the rack, Bassanio? Then confess
What treason there is mingled with your love.

ACT THREE, Scene 2

BASSANIO, PORTIA, GRATIANO, *and* NERISSA *enter with all their attendants, including a* SINGER.

PORTIA

(to BASSANIO*)* Please wait a day or two before making your choice. If you choose wrong, I'll lose your company. So wait a while. Something tells me—not love, but something—that I don't want to lose you, and you know that if I hated you I wouldn't think that. But let me put it more clearly in case you don't understand—though I know girls aren't supposed to express their thoughts—I'm just saying I'd like you to stay here for a month or two before you undergo the test for me. I could tell you how to choose correctly, but then I'd be disregarding the oath I took. So I'll never tell. But you might lose me by making the wrong choice. If you do choose wrong, you'll make me wish for something very bad. I'd wish I had ignored my oath and told you everything. God, your eyes have bewitched me. They've divided me in two. One half of me is yours, and the other half—my own half, I'd call it—belongs to you too. If it's mine, then it's yours, and so I'm all yours. But in this awful day and age people don't even have the right to their own property! So though I'm yours, I'm not yours. If there's no chance for me to be yours, then it's just bad luck. I know I'm talking too much, but I do that just to make the time last longer, and to postpone your test.

BASSANIO

Let me choose now. I feel tortured by all this talking.

PORTIA

Portia and Bassanio are role-playing here, pretending to be torturer and victim.

Tortured, Bassanio? Then confess to your crime. Tell us about the treason you've mixed in with your love.

BASSANIO
    None but that ugly treason of mistrust
    Which makes me fear th' enjoying of my love.
30   There may as well be amity and life
    'Tween snow and fire, as treason and my love.

PORTIA
    Ay, but I fear you speak upon the rack
    Where men enforcèd do speak anything.

BASSANIO
    Promise me life, and I'll confess the truth.

PORTIA
35   Well then, confess and live.

BASSANIO
                         "Confess and love"
    Had been the very sum of my confession.
    O happy torment, when my torturer
    Doth teach me answers for deliverance!
    But let me to my fortune and the caskets.

PORTIA
40   Away, then. I am locked in one of them.
    If you do love me you will find me out.—
    Nerissa and the rest, stand all aloof.
    Let music sound while he doth make his choice.
    Then if he lose he makes a swanlike end,
45   Fading in music. That the comparison
    May stand more proper, my eye shall be the stream
    And watery deathbed for him. He may win,
    And what is music then? Then music is
    Even as the flourish when true subjects bow
50   To a new-crownèd monarch. Such it is
    As are those dulcet sounds in break of day
    That creep into the dreaming bridegroom's ear
    And summon him to marriage.

BASSANIO

The only treason I'm guilty of is worrying that I'm never going to get to enjoy you. Treason has nothing at all to do with my love. They're as opposite as hot and cold.

PORTIA

Hmmm, I'm not sure I believe what you're saying. Men under torture will confess anything.

BASSANIO

Promise me you'll let me live, and I'll confess the truth.

PORTIA

All right then, confess and live.

BASSANIO

"Confess and love" is more like it. Oh, torture's fun when my torturer tells me what I have to say to go free! But let me try my luck on the boxes.

PORTIA

Go ahead, then. I'm locked in one of them. If you really love me, you'll find me.—Nerissa and the rest of you, get away from him. Play some music while he chooses. Then if he loses, it'll be his swan song, music before the end. And since swans need water to swim in, I'll cry him a river when he loses. But on the other hand, he may win. What music should we play then? If he wins, the music should be like the majestic trumpets that blare when subjects bow to a newly crowned monarch. It's the sweet sounds at daybreak that the dreaming bridegroom hears on his wedding morning, calling him to the church.

ACT THREE

                                   Now he goes
                     With no less presence but with much more love
55   Than young Alcides, when he did redeem
                     The virgin tribute paid by howling Troy
                     To the sea monster. I stand for sacrifice.
                     The rest aloof are the Dardanian wives,
                     With blearèd visages come forth to view
60   The issue of th' exploit.—Go, Hercules!
                     Live thou, I live. With much, much more dismay
                     I view the fight than thou that makest the fray.

                     A song, the whilst BASSANIO *comments on the caskets to himself*

SINGER
          (sings)
                         Tell me where is fancy bred.
                         Or in the heart or in the head?
65   *How begot, how nourishèd?*
ALL
          Reply, reply.
SINGER
          (sings)
                         It is engendered in the eyes,
                         With gazing fed, and fancy dies
                         In the cradle where it lies.
70   *Let us all ring fancy's knell*
                         I'll begin it.—Ding, dong, bell.
ALL
          Ding, dong, bell.

Bassanio's walking to the boxes now. He looks as dignified as Hercules did when he saved the princess Hesione from the sea monster. But he loves me more than Hercules loved the princess. I'll play Hesione, and everyone else will be the bystanders watching with tear-streaked faces. We've all come out to see what will happen.—Go, Hercules! If you survive, I'll live. I'm more anxious watching you fight than you are in the fight itself.

A song plays while BASSANIO *mulls over the boxes.*

SINGER

(singing)
  Tell me where do our desires start,
  In the heart or in the head?
  How are they created, how sustained?

ALL

  Answer me, answer me.

SINGER

(singing)
  Desires start in the eyes,
  Sustained by gazing, and desires die
  Very young.
  Let's all mourn our dead desires.
  I'll begin—Ding, dong, bell.

ALL

  Ding, dong, bell.

ACT THREE

BASSANIO

So may the outward shows be least themselves.
The world is still deceived with ornament.
75 In law, what plea so tainted and corrupt
But, being seasoned with a gracious voice,
Obscures the show of evil? In religion,
What damnèd error, but some sober brow
Will bless it and approve it with a text,
80 Hiding the grossness with fair ornament?
There is no vice so simple but assumes
Some mark of virtue on his outward parts.
How many cowards whose hearts are all as false
As stairs of sand wear yet upon their chins
85 The beards of Hercules and frowning Mars,
Who, inward searched, have livers white as milk,
And these assume but valor's excrement
To render them redoubted. Look on beauty,
And you shall see 'tis purchased by the weight,
90 Which therein works a miracle in nature,
Making them lightest that wear most of it.
So are those crispèd snaky golden locks
Which maketh such wanton gambols with the wind,
Upon supposèd fairness, often known
95 To be the dowry of a second head,
The skull that bred them in the sepulcher.
Thus ornament is but the guilèd shore
To a most dangerous sea, the beauteous scarf
Veiling an Indian beauty—in a word,
100 The seeming truth which cunning times put on
To entrap the wisest. Therefore then, thou gaudy gold,
Hard food for Midas, I will none of thee.
Nor none of thee, thou pale and common drudge
'Tween man and man. But thou, thou meagre lead,
105 Which rather threaten'st than dost promise aught,
Thy paleness moves me more than eloquence,
And here choose I. Joy be the consequence!

BASSANIO

You can't always judge a book by its cover. People are often tricked by false appearances. In court, someone can deliver a false plea but hide its wickedness with a pretty voice. In religion, don't serious men defend sins with Scripture, covering up evil with a show of good. Every sin in the world manages to make itself look good somehow. How many people are cowards at heart but wear beards like Hercules or Mars, the god of war? Take another example: beauty. It can be bought by the ounce in makeup, which works miracles. Women who wear it the most are respected the least. It's the same thing with hair. Curly golden hair moves so nicely in the wind and makes a woman beautiful. But you can buy that kind of hair as a wig, and wigs are made from dead people's hair. Decoration's nothing but a danger, meant to trick and trap the viewer. A lovely, cunning shore can distract a man from the perils of a stormy sea, just as a pretty scarf can hide a dangerous dark-skinned beauty. Nowadays, everyone's fooled by appearances. So I'll have nothing to do with that gaudy gold box—it's like the gold that Midas couldn't eat. And I'll have nothing to do with the pale silver either, the metal that common coins are made of. But this humble lead one, though it looks too threatening to promise me anything good, moves me more than I can say. So this is the one I choose. I hope I'm happy with my choice!

PORTIA

    (aside) How all the other passions fleet to air,
    As doubtful thoughts, and rash-embraced despair,
110   And shuddering fear, and green-eyed jealousy!
    O love, be moderate. Allay thy ecstasy.
    In measure rein thy joy. Scant this excess.
    I feel too much thy blessing. Make it less,
    For fear I surfeit.

BASSANIO

    (opening the lead casket)
               What find I here?
115   Fair Portia's counterfeit! What demigod
    Hath come so near creation? Move these eyes?
    Or whether, riding on the balls of mine,
    Seem they in motion? Here are severed lips,
    Parted with sugar breath. So sweet a bar
120   Should sunder such sweet friends. Here in her hairs,
    The painter plays the spider and hath woven
    A golden mesh t' entrap the hearts of men
    Faster than gnats in cobwebs. But her eyes—
    How could he see to do them? Having made one,
125   Methinks it should have power to steal both his
    And leave itself unfurnished. Yet look how far
    The substance of my praise doth wrong this shadow
    In underprizing it, so far this shadow
    Doth limp behind the substance. Here's the scroll,
130   The continent and summary of my fortune.
    (reads)
        "You that choose not by the view,
        Chance as fair and choose as true.
        Since this fortune falls to you,
        Be content and seek no new.
135   If you be well pleased with this
        And hold your fortune for your bliss,
        Turn you where your lady is
        And claim her with a loving kiss."

PORTIA

(to herself) All my other emotions are vanishing into thin air, as all my doubts and desperation and fears and jealousy are all flying away! Oh, I need to calm down, make my love and my joy less intense. I'm feeling this too strongly. Please make my love less, or I'm going to overindulge, making myself sick.

BASSANIO

(opening the lead box) What do we have here? A picture of beautiful Portia! What artist captured her likeness so well? Are these eyes moving? Or do they just seem to move as my eyes move? Her sweet breath forces her lips open, a lovely divider of lovely lips. And look at her hair, looking like a golden mesh to trap the hearts of men, like little flies in a cobweb. The painter was like a spider in creating it so delicately. But her eyes— how could he keep looking at them long enough to paint them? I would've expected that when he finished one of them, it would have enraptured him and kept him from painting the other. But I'm giving only faint praise of the picture, just as the picture, as good as it is, is only a faint imitation of the real woman herself. Here's the scroll that sums up my fate:
(he reads)
    "You who don't judge by looks alone,
    Have better luck, and make the right choice.
    Since this prize is yours,
    Be happy with it, and don't look for a new one.
    If you're happy with what you've won
    And accept this prize as your blissful destiny,
    Then turn to where your lady is,
    And claim her with a loving kiss."

ACT THREE

A gentle scroll. Fair lady, by your leave,
140 I come by note to give and to receive.
Like one of two contending in a prize
That thinks he hath done well in people's eyes,
Hearing applause and universal shout,
Giddy in spirit, still gazing in a doubt
145 Whether these pearls of praise be his or no—
So, thrice-fair lady, stand I even so,
As doubtful whether what I see be true
Until confirmed, signed, ratified by you.

PORTIA
You see me, Lord Bassanio, where I stand
150 Such as I am. Though for myself alone
I would not be ambitious in my wish
To wish myself much better, yet for you
I would be trebled twenty times myself—
A thousand times more fair, ten thousand times more rich—
155 That only to stand high in your account
I might in virtue, beauties, livings, friends
Exceed account. But the full sum of me
Is sum of something which, to term in gross,
Is an unlessoned girl, unschooled, unpracticèd;
160 Happy in this—she is not yet so old
But she may learn. Happier than this—
She is not bred so dull but she can learn.
Happiest of all is that her gentle spirit
Commits itself to yours to be directed
165 As from her lord, her governor, her king.
Myself and what is mine to you and yours
Is now converted. But now I was the lord
Of this fair mansion, master of my servants,
Queen o'er myself. And even now, but now,
170 This house, these servants, and this same myself
Are yours, my lord's. I give them with this ring,
Which when you part from, lose, or give away,
Let it presage the ruin of your love

A nice message. My lady, with your permission, this note authorizes me to give myself to you with a kiss. But I'm in a daze, like someone who's just won a contest and thinks that all the applause and cheering is for him, but isn't sure yet. And so, beautiful lady, I'm standing here just like that, wondering whether all this can be true until you tell me it is.

PORTIA

You see me standing here, Lord Bassanio. What you see is what you get. Though I wouldn't wish to be better for my own sake, for your sake I wish I were twenty times more than myself—a thousand times more beautiful and ten thousand times richer—just so you might value me more, so my good qualities, beauty, possessions, and friends would be more than you could calculate. What you're getting is an innocent and inexperienced girl. I'm happy that at least I'm not too old to learn new things. I'm even happier that I'm not stupid, and I can learn. I'm happiest of all that I'm yours now, my lord, my king, and you can guide me as you wish. Everything I am and everything I have now belongs to you. Just a minute ago I was the owner of this beautiful mansion, master of these servants, and queen over myself. But as of right this second all these things are yours. With this ring I give them all to you.

And be my vantage to exclaim on you.
(gives BASSANIO a ring)

BASSANIO

175 Madam, you have bereft me of all words.
Only my blood speaks to you in my veins.
And there is such confusion in my powers
As after some oration fairly spoke
By a belovèd prince there doth appear
180 Among the buzzing pleasèd multitude,
Where every something, being blent together,
Turns to a wild of nothing, save of joy,
Expressed and not expressed. But when this ring
Parts from this finger, then parts life from hence.
185 O, then be bold to say Bassanio's dead!

NERISSA

My lord and lady, it is now our time,
That have stood by and seen our wishes prosper,
To cry, "Good joy, good joy, my lord and lady!"

GRATIANO

My Lord Bassanio and my gentle lady,
190 I wish you all the joy that you can wish,
For I am sure you can wish none from me.
And when your honors mean to solemnize
The bargain of your faith, I do beseech you
Even at that time I may be married too.

BASSANIO

195 With all my heart, so thou canst get a wife.

GRATIANO

I thank your lordship, you have got me one.
My eyes, my lord, can look as swift as yours.
You saw the mistress, I beheld the maid.
You loved, I loved. For intermission
200 No more pertains to me, my lord, than you.
Your fortune stood upon the casket there,
And so did mine too, as the matter falls.

If you ever give away this ring or lose it, it means our love's doomed, and I'll have a right to be angry with you. *(she gives* BASSANIO *the ring)*

BASSANIO

Madam, you've left me speechless, but my feelings are responding to your words. I'm as confused as a crowd of people going wild after hearing their prince give a speech. But the day I take this ring off will be the day I die. If you see me without it, you can be confident I'm dead.

NERISSA

My lord and lady, it's now our turn, who have been watching as our dreams came true. Now we can shout, "Congratulations, congratulations, my lord and lady!"

GRATIANO

My Lord Bassanio, and my dear lady, I wish you all the joy I can wish for. And when you get married, I hope I can be married at the same time.

BASSANIO

Absolutely, if you can find a wife by then.

GRATIANO

I think I've found one already, thanks to you, my lord. I can fall in love just as quickly as you can, and I loved Nerissa as soon as I laid eyes on her. You fell in love with Portia, and I fell in love with Nerissa, because I'm not in the habit of delaying any more than you are, my lord. Your fate depended on those boxes, and it turns out that mine did too. I couldn't help but chase

For wooing here until I sweat again,
And swearing till my very roof was dry
205 With oaths of love, at last—if promise last—
I got a promise of this fair one here
To have her love, provided that your fortune
Achieved her mistress.

PORTIA
                                        Is this true, Nerissa?

NERISSA
Madam, it is, so you stand pleased withal.

BASSANIO
210 And do you, Gratiano, mean good faith?

GRATIANO
Yes, faith, my lord.

BASSANIO
Our feast shall be much honored in your marriage.

GRATIANO
(to NERISSA*)* We'll play with them the first boy for a
thousand ducats.

NERISSA
215 What, and stake down?

GRATIANO
No, we shall ne'er win at that sport and stake down.
But who comes here? Lorenzo and his infidel? What, and
my old Venetian friend Salerio?

Enter LORENZO, JESSICA, *and* SALERIO, *a messenger from
Venice*

BASSANIO
Lorenzo and Salerio, welcome hither,
220 If that the youth of my new interest here
Have power to bid you welcome.

her. I started making love vows to her till my mouth was dry. Then finally she said she loved me and would marry me if you two got married as well.

PORTIA

Is that true, Nerissa?

NERISSA

Yes, madam, it is, if it's all right with you.

BASSANIO

And do you mean what you're saying, Gratiano?

GRATIANO

Yes, my lord.

BASSANIO

Then we'd be honored to have you join us in our wedding ceremony.

GRATIANO

(to **NERISSA***)* Let's bet them a thousand ducats that we will have a son first.

NERISSA

You want to stake the money down now?

GRATIANO

Hey, if I lay down my "stake," I'll never be able to have a son. But who's this coming? Lorenzo and his pagan girlfriend? What, and my old Venetian friend Salerio?

Gratiano puns on "stake" as both money that is bet and penis.

LORENZO *and* **JESSICA** *enter with* **SALERIO***, a messenger from Venice.*

BASSANIO

Welcome, Lorenzo and Salerio. I hope my position in this new house is firm enough to allow me the right to welcome my friends.

ACT THREE

(to PORTIA*)*

By your leave,
I bid my very friends and countrymen,
Sweet Portia, welcome.

PORTIA

So do I, my lord.
They are entirely welcome.

LORENZO

225 *(to* BASSANIO*)* I thank your honor. For my part, my lord,
My purpose was not to have seen you here.
But meeting with Salerio by the way,
He did entreat me, past all saying nay,
To come with him along.

SALERIO

I did, my lord.
230 And I have reason for it. Signor Antonio
Commends him to you.
(gives BASSANIO *a letter)*

BASSANIO

Ere I ope his letter,
I pray you tell me how my good friend doth.

SALERIO

Not sick, my lord, unless it be in mind,
Nor well, unless in mind. His letter there
235 Will show you his estate.

BASSANIO *opens the letter and reads it*

GRATIANO

(indicating JESSICA*)*
Nerissa, cheer yond stranger. Bid her welcome.—
Your hand, Salerio. What's the news from Venice?
How doth that royal merchant, good Antonio?
I know he will be glad of our success.
240 We are the Jasons, we have won the fleece.

(to PORTIA*)* With your permission, Portia, I welcome my good friends and countrymen.

PORTIA

I do too, my lord. They're entirely welcome.

LORENZO

(to BASSANIO*)* Thank you, sir. I didn't intend to come see you. But I ran into Salerio on the way, and he begged me to come along with him until I couldn't say no.

SALERIO

That's true, and with good reason. This letter is for you from Signor Antonio. *(he gives* BASSANIO *a letter)*

BASSANIO

Before I open this letter, please tell me how my good friend is doing.

SALERIO

He's not sick, my lord, but he's very upset, and his problems are serious. His letter will tell you how he's doing.

BASSANIO *opens the letter and reads it.*

GRATIANO

(pointing at JESSICA*)* Nerissa, welcome this stranger. —Salerio, welcome. Any news from Venice? How's the great merchant Antonio doing? I know he'll be happy to hear of our success. We're like the ancient hero Jason, we went looking for the Golden Fleece and we won it!

SALERIO
    I would you had won the fleece that he hath lost.

PORTIA
    There are some shrewd contents in yond same paper
    That steals the color from Bassanio's cheek.
    Some dear friend dead, else nothing in the world
245   Could turn so much the constitution
    Of any constant man. What, worse and worse?—
    With leave, Bassanio, I am half yourself,
    And I must freely have the half of anything
    That this same paper brings you.

BASSANIO
                      O sweet Portia,
250   Here are a few of the unpleasant'st words
    That ever blotted paper. Gentle lady,
    When I did first impart my love to you,
    I freely told you, all the wealth I had
    Ran in my veins. I was a gentleman,
255   And then I told you true. And yet, dear lady,
    Rating myself at nothing, you shall see
    How much I was a braggart. When I told you
    My state was nothing, I should then have told you
    That I was worse than nothing, for indeed
260   I have engaged myself to a dear friend,
    Engaged my friend to his mere enemy
    To feed my means.
                Here is a letter, lady,
    The paper as the body of my friend,
    And every word in it a gaping wound,
265   Issuing life blood.—But is it true, Salerio?
    Have all his ventures failed? What, not one hit?
    From Tripolis, from Mexico and England,
    From Lisbon, Barbary, and India?
    And not one vessel 'scape the dreadful touch
270   Of merchant-marring rocks?

SALERIO

I wish you'd won the fleece he lost.

Salerio puns on "fleece" (the wool from a ram) and "fleets" (groups of ships).

PORTIA

Something bad in that letter is making Bassanio turn pale. Some good friend of his must have died, because nothing else in the world could change a man so much. What, does the news only get worse?—Please, Bassanio, I'm half of you, so let me bear half the burden this letter brings you.

BASSANIO

Oh Portia, these are some of the worst words that ever stained a piece of paper. My darling, when I gave my love to you, I told you that all the wealth I had ran within my veins—that I have noble blood, but no money. When I said that, I told you the truth. But my dear, when I said I was worth nothing, I was actually bragging—I should've said that I was worse than nothing. I've borrowed money from a dear friend who in turn borrowed money from his mortal enemy for my sake. Here's a letter, my dear. The paper's like my friend's body, and every word in it is a bleeding wound on that body.—But is it true, Salerio? Have all his business ventures failed? Not even one success? He had ships to Tripolis, Mexico, England, Lisbon, North Africa, and India, and not one of these ships avoided the rocks?

ACT THREE

SALERIO

                              Not one, my lord.
Besides, it should appear that if he had
The present money to discharge the Jew,
He would not take it. Never did I know
A creature that did bear the shape of man
275 So keen and greedy to confound a man.
He plies the duke at morning and at night,
And doth impeach the freedom of the state
If they deny him justice. Twenty merchants,
The duke himself, and the magnificoes
280 Of greatest port have all persuaded with him.
But none can drive him from the envious plea
Of forfeiture, of justice, and his bond.

JESSICA

When I was with him I have heard him swear
To Tubal and to Chus, his countrymen,
285 That he would rather have Antonio's flesh
Than twenty times the value of the sum
That he did owe him. And I know, my lord,
If law, authority, and power deny not,
It will go hard with poor Antonio.

PORTIA

290 Is it your dear friend that is thus in trouble?

BASSANIO

The dearest friend to me, the kindest man,
The best conditioned and unwearied spirit
In doing courtesies, and one in whom
The ancient Roman honor more appears
295 Than any that draws breath in Italy.

PORTIA

What sum owes he the Jew?

BASSANIO

For me, three thousand ducats.

SALERIO

Not one, my lord. Anyway, even if he had the money now, the Jew probably wouldn't take it. I've never seen a creature with a human shape who was so eager to destroy a man. He's at the duke's morning and night, accusing the state of harming free trade if they deny him justice. Twenty merchants, the duke himself, and the highest-ranking Venetian nobles have all tried to persuade him to forget his contract, but nobody can do it. He's determined to get the penalty specified in his contract with Antonio.

JESSICA

When I was still living with him I heard him swear to Tubal and Cush, his countrymen, that he'd rather have Antonio's flesh than twenty times the sum Antonio owed. And I know that unless the law intervenes, it'll be bad news for poor Antonio.

PORTIA

Is this your good friend who's in so much trouble?

BASSANIO

Yes, he's my best friend, the kindest man and most courteous to others. He's more honorable than anyone else in Italy.

PORTIA

How much does he owe the Jew?

BASSANIO

Three thousand ducats.

PORTIA

What, no more?
Pay him six thousand and deface the bond!
Double six thousand, and then treble that,
300 Before a friend of this description
Shall lose a hair through Bassanio's fault.
First go with me to church and call me wife,
And then away to Venice to your friend.
For never shall you lie by Portia's side
305 With an unquiet soul. You shall have gold
To pay the petty debt twenty times over.
When it is paid, bring your true friend along.
My maid Nerissa and myself meantime
Will live as maids and widows. Come, away!
310 For you shall hence upon your wedding day.
Bid your friends welcome, show a merry cheer.
Since you are dear bought, I will love you dear.
But let me hear the letter of your friend.

BASSANIO

(reads)

"Sweet Bassanio, my ships have all miscarried. My
315 creditors grow cruel. My estate is very low. My bond
to the Jew is forfeit. And since in paying it, it is
impossible I should live, all debts are cleared between
you and I if I might but see you at my death.
Notwithstanding, use your pleasure. If your love do
320 not persuade you to come, let not my letter."

PORTIA

O love, dispatch all business and be gone!

BASSANIO

Since I have your good leave to go away,
I will make haste. But till I come again,
No bed shall e'er be guilty of my stay,
325 No rest be interposer 'twixt us twain.

Exeunt

PORTIA

What, that's all? Pay him six thousand and cancel the debt. I'd pay twelve thousand before I'd let a friend like that suffer in the slightest because of you. First come with me to church to get married. Then you can leave for Venice to see your friend. You have to go, because you'll never sleep next to me peacefully without settling this. I'll give you enough gold to pay back your debt twenty times over. When it's paid, bring your friend back. Until you get back, Nerissa and I will live like virgins and widows. Come on, let's go, because you're going to leave me the same day we get married. Put on a happy face, and welcome your friends. Since it's costing me a lot to marry you, I'll think of you as even more precious. But let me hear the letter from your friend.

BASSANIO

(he reads)

"Dear Bassanio, my ships have all been wrecked. My creditors are getting mean. My money's almost run out. I couldn't pay my debt to the Jew on the due date. Since I'll certainly die when he takes his collateral out of my flesh, all debts are cleared between you and me if I can just see you again before I die. In any case, do what you want. If your affection for me doesn't convince you to come, don't let my letter do so."

PORTIA

Oh, my darling, make your arrangements and go!

BASSANIO

Since you're letting me leave, I'll hurry. But I won't sleep till I get back.

They exit.

ACT THREE, Scene 3

Enter SHYLOCK, SOLANIO, ANTONIO, *and the jailer*

SHYLOCK
Jailer, look to him. Tell not me of mercy.
This is the fool that lent out money gratis.
Jailer, look to him.

ANTONIO
Hear me yet, good Shylock.

SHYLOCK
I'll have my bond. Speak not against my bond.
5 I have sworn an oath that I will have my bond.
Thou calledst me dog before thou hadst a cause.
But since I am a dog, beware my fangs.
The duke shall grant me justice.—I do wonder,
Thou naughty jailer, that thou art so fond
10 To come abroad with him at his request.

ANTONIO
I pray thee, hear me speak.

SHYLOCK
I'll have my bond. I will not hear thee speak.
I'll have my bond, and therefore speak no more.
I'll not be made a soft and dull-eyed fool
15 To shake the head, relent and sigh, and yield
To Christian intercessors. Follow not.
I'll have no speaking. I will have my bond.

Exit SHYLOCK

SOLANIO
It is the most impenetrable cur
That ever kept with men.

ACT THREE, Scene 3

SHYLOCK, SOLANIO, ANTONIO, *and the jailer enter.*

SHYLOCK

Jailer, watch out for this one. Don't try to convince me to feel sorry for him. This is the fool who lent out money without charging interest. Jailer, keep an eye on him.

ANTONIO

Listen to me, good Shylock.

SHYLOCK

Shylock uses the word "bond" here to mean the goods Antonio promised to give Shylock if he defaulted on the loan—in other words, the pound of Antonio's flesh.

I'm going to get my bond. Don't try to say anything against my taking my bond. I've sworn an oath that I will have my bond. You called me a dog before you had any reason to. But since I'm a dog, beware my fangs. The duke will give me justice.—I do wonder, jailer, how you can be so foolish as to let this prisoner out of his cell.

ANTONIO

Please, listen to me.

SHYLOCK

I want my bond. I won't listen to you. I want my bond, so stop talking. I won't be taken for a fool who sighs and gives in to Christian meddlers. Don't follow me. I'm not talking with you. I want my bond.

He exits.

SOLANIO

He's the most stubborn dog that ever lived among humans.

ANTONIO
                              Let him alone.
20 I'll follow him no more with bootless prayers.
He seeks my life. His reason well I know.
I oft delivered from his forfeitures
Many that have at times made moan to me.
Therefore he hates me.

SOLANIO
                              I am sure the duke
25 Will never grant this forfeiture to hold.

ANTONIO
The duke cannot deny the course of law.
For the commodity that strangers have
With us in Venice, if it be denied,
Will much impeach the justice of his state,
30 Since that the trade and profit of the city
Consisteth of all nations. Therefore go.
These griefs and losses have so bated me,
That I shall hardly spare a pound of flesh
Tomorrow to my bloody creditor.—
35 Well, jailer, on.—Pray God Bassanio come
To see me pay his debt, and then I care not.

Exeunt

ANTONIO

Leave him alone. I won't follow him around with useless pleas anymore. He wants me dead. I know the real reason. I've often given money to people who were unable to pay back their loans to him. That's why he hates me.

SOLANIO

I'm sure the duke will never allow this contract to be enforced.

ANTONIO

The duke can't deny the law, because that would threaten the security of all foreign merchants in Venice, and that's how the city makes its money. If the government disregards the law, it will be discredited. So go. I've lost so much weight worrying about my losses that I'll hardly have a pound of flesh to spare for my bloody creditor tomorrow.—Well, jailer, let's go.—I hope to God that Bassanio comes to see me pay his debt. After that, I don't care what happens.

They exit.

ACT THREE, Scene 4

Enter PORTIA, NERISSA, LORENZO, JESSICA, *and* BALTHAZAR, *a man of* PORTIA'*s*

LORENZO

Madam, although I speak it in your presence,
You have a noble and a true conceit
Of godlike amity, which appears most strongly
In bearing thus the absence of your lord.
5   But if you knew to whom you show this honor,
How true a gentleman you send relief,
How dear a lover of my lord your husband,
I know you would be prouder of the work
Than customary bounty can enforce you.

PORTIA

10   I never did repent for doing good,
Nor shall not now; for in companions
That do converse and waste the time together
Whose souls do bear an equal yoke of love,
There must be needs a like proportion
15   Of lineaments, of manners, and of spirit,
Which makes me think that this Antonio,
Being the bosom lover of my lord,
Must needs be like my lord. If it be so,
How little is the cost I have bestowed
20   In purchasing the semblance of my soul
From out the state of hellish cruelty!
This comes too near the praising of myself.
Therefore no more of it. Hear other things.
Lorenzo, I commit into your hands
25   The husbandry and manage of my house
Until my lord's return.

ACT THREE, Scene 4

PORTIA, NERISSA, LORENZO, *and* JESSICA *enter with*
BALTHAZAR, *a servant of* PORTIA'S.

LORENZO

Madam, I hope you don't mind my saying that I
admire your noble respect for friendship, which you
show in letting your husband go off to help his friend
like this. If you only knew the man you're helping out,
and what a faithful gentleman he is and how much he
loves your husband, I know you'd be even prouder of
your kindness than you normally might be.

PORTIA

I've never regretted doing good, and I don't now.
Friends who spend a lot of time together and really
care equally for each other must have many traits in
common. Since Antonio's my husband's best friend,
they must be very similar men. In that case, the money
I've sent is a small price to pay to rescue someone who
resembles my Bassanio, who's like my own soul.—
Anyway, let's change the subject, since I feel like I'm
starting to flatter myself. I have a favor to ask of you.
Lorenzo, please take charge of the management of my
house until my husband comes back.

ACT THREE

         For mine own part,
I have toward heaven breathed a secret vow
To live in prayer and contemplation,
Only attended by Nerissa here
30 Until her husband and my lord's return.
There is a monastery two miles off,
And there will we abide. I do desire you
Not to deny this imposition,
The which my love and some necessity
35 Now lays upon you.

LORENZO
         Madam, with all my heart.
I shall obey you in all fair commands.

PORTIA
My people do already know my mind
And will acknowledge you and Jessica
In place of Lord Bassanio and myself.
40 So fare you well till we shall meet again.

LORENZO
Fair thoughts and happy hours attend on you!

JESSICA
I wish your ladyship all heart's content.

PORTIA
I thank you for your wish, and am well pleased
To wish it back on you. Fare you well, Jessica.

       Exeunt JESSICA *and* LORENZO

45 Now, Balthazar,
As I have ever found thee honest true,
So let me find thee still.
(gives BALTHAZAR *a letter)*
        Take this same letter,
And use thou all th' endeavour of a man
In speed to Padua. See thou render this
50 Into my cousin's hands, Doctor Bellario.

I've sworn to God that I'll live a life of prayer and contemplation until my husband returns. Only Nerissa will keep me company. There's a monastery two miles away where we can stay. Please say you'll agree, because I really need you to do this.

LORENZO

Madam, with all my heart. I'll do anything you ask.

PORTIA

I've already spoken to my staff about this. They'll consider you and Jessica masters of this house in place of Lord Bassanio and myself. So goodbye until we meet again.

LORENZO

I hope you can relax and enjoy yourself!

JESSICA

I hope you find peace and happiness, my lady.

PORTIA

Thank you. I wish you the same. Goodbye, Jessica.

JESSICA *and* LORENZO *exit.*

Now, Balthazar, you've always been honest and faithful to me, and I trust you still are. *(she gives* BALTHAZAR *a letter)* Take this letter to Padua as fast as you can. Make sure you put it into the hands of my cousin Bellario, the Doctor of Laws.

And look what notes and garments he doth give thee,
Bring them, I pray thee, with imagined speed
Unto the traject, to the common ferry
Which trades to Venice. Waste no time in words,
55   But get thee gone. I shall be there before thee.

BALTHAZAR
Madam, I go with all convenient speed.

Exit **BALTHAZAR**

PORTIA
Come on, Nerissa, I have work in hand
That you yet know not of. We'll see our husbands
Before they think of us.

NERISSA
                                      Shall they see us?

PORTIA
60   They shall, Nerissa, but in such a habit
That they shall think we are accomplishèd
With that we lack. I'll hold thee any wager,
When we are both accoutred like young men,
I'll prove the prettier fellow of the two,
65   And wear my dagger with the braver grace,
And speak between the change of man and boy
With a reed voice, and turn two mincing steps
Into a manly stride, and speak of frays
Like a fine bragging youth, and tell quaint lies,
70   How honorable ladies sought my love,
Which I denying, they fell sick and died—
I could not do withal!—Then I'll repent
And wish for all that, that I had not killed them.
And twenty of these puny lies I'll tell,
75   That men shall swear I have discontinued school
Above a twelvemonth. I have within my mind
A thousand raw tricks of these bragging jacks
Which I will practice.

And as quickly as possible, take whatever letters and clothes he gives you to the public ferry that goes back and forth to Venice. Don't waste time talking now. Just go. I'll meet you at the ferry.

BALTHAZAR

I'll go as fast as I can, madam.

He exits.

PORTIA

Come on, Nerissa, I have many things to do that you don't even know about yet. We'll see our husbands before they even have a chance to miss us.

NERISSA

Will they see us?

PORTIA

They will, Nerissa, but we'll be disguised as men. I'll bet you anything that I'll be handsomer than you when we're both dressed up. I'll wear my sword more gracefully, and speak like a teenage boy, and walk with a manly stride rather than my ladylike steps. I'll talk about fights like a bragging youth, and I'll tell cute lies about honorable ladies who fell in love with me and got sick and died when I rejected them. They just died, what could I do! Then I'll start feeling sorry for them, wishing I hadn't killed them. I'll tell twenty lies like that, so men will think I graduated from school at least a year ago. I know a thousand immature tricks like that, and I'll use them all.

ACT THREE

NERISSA
Why, shall we turn to men?

PORTIA
80   Fie, what a question's that
If thou wert near a lewd interpreter!
But come, I'll tell thee all my whole device
When I am in my coach, which stays for us
At the park gate. And therefore haste away,
85   For we must measure twenty miles today.

Exeunt

NERISSA

Why, are we turning to men?

PORTIA

What kind of question is that! If I had a dirty mind, I'd think you meant turning to men for sex. Here, I'll tell you my whole plan in my carriage, which is waiting for us at the gate. So hurry up, because we have twenty miles to cover today.

They exit.

ACT THREE, Scene 5

Enter LAUNCELOT *the clown and* JESSICA

LAUNCELOT
Yes, truly, for look you, the sins of the father are to be laid
upon the children. Therefore I promise ye I fear you. I
was always plain with you, and so now I speak my
agitation of the matter. Therefore be o' good cheer, for
5 truly I think you are damned. There is but one hope in it
that can do you any good, and that is but a kind of bastard
hope neither.

JESSICA
And what hope is that, I pray thee?

LAUNCELOT
Marry, you may partly hope that your father got you not,
10 that you are not the Jew's daughter.

JESSICA
That were a kind of bastard hope indeed. So the sins of my
mother should be visited upon me.

LAUNCELOT
Truly then I fear you are damned both by father and
mother. Thus when I shun Scylla your father, I fall into
15 Charybdis your mother. Well, you are gone both ways.

JESSICA
I shall be saved by my husband. He hath made me a
Christian.

LAUNCELOT
Truly, the more to blame he. We were Christians eno'
before, e'en as many as could well live one by another.
20 This making Christians will raise the price of hogs. If we
grow all to be pork-eaters, we shall not shortly have a
rasher on the coals for money.

Enter LORENZO

ACT THREE, Scene 5

LAUNCELOT *and* JESSICA *enter.*

LAUNCELOT

> Yes, look, it's true that children are punished for the sins of their fathers. That's why I'm worried about you. I've always been straightforward with you, so now I'm telling you what I think. Cheer up, because I think you're going to hell. There's only one hope for you, and even that's a kind of illegitimate hope.

JESSICA

> What hope is that, may I ask?

LAUNCELOT

> You can hope your father isn't your real father. Maybe your mother fooled around, and you aren't the Jew's daughter.

JESSICA

> That really is an illegitimate hope. Then I'd be punished for the sins of my mother.

LAUNCELOT

> In that case I'm afraid you're damned by both your father and your mother. When you avoid one trap, you fall into another. You're in trouble either way.

JESSICA

> My husband will save me. He's made me a Christian.

LAUNCELOT

> He was wrong to do that. There were enough Christians before—as many of them as could stand to live near each other. All these new Christians will make the price of hogs go up. If we're all pork-eaters, we won't be able to get our hands on a slice of bacon, even if we've got the money for it.

LORENZO *enters.*

JESSICA
I'll tell my husband, Launcelot, what you say. Here he comes.

LORENZO
25   I shall grow jealous of you shortly, Launcelot, if you thus get my wife into corners.

JESSICA
Nay, you need not fear us, Lorenzo. Launcelot and I are out. He tells me flatly there is no mercy for me in heaven because I am a Jew's daughter, and he says you are no
30   good member of the commonwealth, for in converting Jews to Christians you raise the price of pork.

LORENZO
I shall answer that better to the commonwealth than you can the getting up of the Negro's belly. The Moor is with child by you, Launcelot.

LAUNCELOT
35   It is much that the Moor should be more than reason. But if she be less than an honest woman, she is indeed more than I took her for.

LORENZO
How every fool can play upon the word! I think the best grace of wit will shortly turn into silence, and discourse
40   grow commendable in none only but parrots. Go in, sirrah. Bid them prepare for dinner.

LAUNCELOT
That is done, sir. They have all stomachs.

JESSICA

I'll tell my husband what you've said, Launcelot. Here he comes.

LORENZO

You're going to make me jealous, Launcelot, if you keep taking my wife into dark corners like this!

JESSICA

No, you don't need to worry about us, Lorenzo. Launcelot and I can't agree on anything. He says I won't get into heaven because I'm a Jew's daughter, and he says you're irresponsible because by converting Jews to Christianity you're raising the price of pork.

LORENZO

Like the prince of Morocco, the servant referred to is a "Moor" or North African, in this case a black woman. Launcelot puns on the words "Moor" and "more."

I can justify that better than you can justify sleeping with Portia's African servant. The Moor is pregnant with your child, Launcelot.

LAUNCELOT

It's too bad there's more of the Moor than there ought to be. Well, even if she's a less than honest woman, she's still a lot *more* respectable than I thought at first.

LORENZO

Any fool can make puns! I think the best sign of intelligence will soon be silence, and talking will only be a good thing for parrots to do. Go in and tell the servants to get ready for dinner.

LAUNCELOT

That's already been done, sir. They're all ready to eat dinner.

LORENZO
Goodly Lord, what a wit-snapper are you! Then bid them
prepare dinner.

LAUNCELOT
45 That is done too, sir. Only "Cover!" is the word.

LORENZO
Will you cover then, sir?

LAUNCELOT
Not so, sir, neither. I know my duty.

LORENZO
Yet more quarreling with occasion! Wilt thou show the
whole wealth of thy wit in an instant? I pray thee,
50 understand a plain man in his plain meaning. Go to thy
fellows, bid them cover the table, serve in the meat, and
we will come in to dinner.

LAUNCELOT
For the table, sir, it shall be served in. For the meat, sir, it
shall be covered. For your coming in to dinner, sir, why,
55 let it be as humours and conceits shall govern.

Exit **LAUNCELOT**

LORENZO
O dear discretion, how his words are suited!
The fool hath planted in his memory
An army of good words, and I do know
A many fools that stand in better place,
60 Garnished like him, that for a tricksy word
Defy the matter. How cheerest thou, Jessica?

LORENZO

Good Lord, what a clown you are! Tell them to *make* the dinner.

LAUNCELOT

That's also been done, sir. The word you're looking for is "cover."

> By "cover," Launcelot means "set the table."

LORENZO

Will you cover, then?

LAUNCELOT

No, sir—I know my duty.

> Launcelot now interprets "cover" to mean put on his hat, which he's not supposed to do in front of his superiors.

LORENZO

You keep finding ways to mock me! Are you planning on showing me all your wit at once? Please understand my simple message: go tell the servants to set the table and bring in the food, and we'll come in to dinner.

LAUNCELOT

About the table, sir, dinner will be served on it. As for the food, it will be served in covered dishes. As for your coming in to dinner, just do what you feel is right.

LAUNCELOT exits.

LORENZO

Oh, he's good at bending words around! The fool has memorized a whole army full of fancy words. I know jesters in better positions, with the same talents he has. They also like to digress from the topic at hand by playing with language. Anyway, how are you, Jessica?

And now, good sweet, say thy opinion.
How dost thou like the Lord Bassanio's wife?

JESSICA
Past all expressing. It is very meet
65 The Lord Bassanio live an upright life,
For having such a blessing in his lady,
He finds the joys of heaven here on earth.
And if on earth he do not merit it,
In reason he should never come to heaven.
70 Why, if two gods should play some heavenly match
And on the wager lay two earthly women,
And Portia one, there must be something else
Pawned with the other, for the poor rude world
Hath not her fellow.

LORENZO
                    Even such a husband
75 Hast thou of me as she is for a wife.

JESSICA
Nay, but ask my opinion too of that!

LORENZO
I will anon. First let us go to dinner.

JESSICA
Nay, let me praise you while I have a stomach.

LORENZO
No, pray thee, let it serve for table talk.
80 Then howsome'er thou speak'st 'mong other things
I shall digest it.

JESSICA
                    Well, I'll set you forth.

Exeunt

And how do you like Lord Bassanio's wife?

JESSICA

I like her more than I can say. Bassanio should live an upstanding life because having a wife like Portia is a blessing. It's as if he found heaven here on earth. And if he doesn't deserve this joy on earth, he'll never deserve it in heaven. Imagine what would happen if two gods in heaven made a bet. If one of them used Portia as his stake, the other god would have a hard time coming up with a human woman to match her value. The poor rude world doesn't have her equal.

LORENZO

As good a wife as she is, that's how good a husband I am to you.

JESSICA

I'll be the judge of that!

LORENZO

I'll give you a chance to judge later. First let's go to dinner.

JESSICA

No, let me say some good things about you while I'm in the mood.

LORENZO

No, please, save it for dinner conversation. That way, no matter what you say, I'll digest it with everything else.

JESSICA

In that case I'll serve you up like a dish of food.

They exit.

ACT FOUR

Scene 1

Enter the DUKE, *the magnificoes,* ANTONIO, BASSANIO, GRATIANO, SALERIO, *and others*

DUKE
What, is Antonio here?

ANTONIO
Ready, so please your grace.

DUKE
I am sorry for thee. Thou art come to answer
A stony adversary, an inhuman wretch
5   Uncapable of pity, void and empty
From any dram of mercy.

ANTONIO
                I have heard
Your grace hath ta'en great pains to qualify
His rigorous course. But since he stands obdurate
And that no lawful means can carry me
10   Out of his envy's reach, I do oppose
My patience to his fury, and am armed
To suffer with a quietness of spirit
The very tyranny and rage of his.

DUKE
Go, one, and call the Jew into the court.

SALERIO
15   He is ready at the door. He comes, my lord.

Enter SHYLOCK

ACT FOUR

Scene 1

The magnificoes are the wealthiest and most important noblemen of Venice, apart from the Duke

The DUKE, *the magnificoes,* ANTONIO, BASSANIO, GRA-
TIANO, SALERIO, *and attendants all enter.*

DUKE

Is Antonio here?

ANTONIO

Yes, sir, I'm here.

DUKE

I feel sorry for you. You've come to face a ruthless enemy, an inhuman wretch incapable of pity, without any feelings of mercy.

ANTONIO

They tell me you've done everything you can to talk him out of what he's doing. But since he remains stubborn, and there's no legal way to protect me from his malice, I'll just have to take what he'll give me. I'm ready to suffer peacefully whatever he does to me in his cruelty and anger.

DUKE

One of you go call the Jew into court here.

SALERIO

He's standing ready outside the door. Here he comes, my lord.

SHYLOCK *enters.*

DUKE
Make room, and let him stand before our face.—
Shylock, the world thinks, and I think so too,
That thou but lead'st this fashion of thy malice
To the last hour of act, and then 'tis thought
20   Thou'lt show thy mercy and remorse more strange
Than is thy strange apparent cruelty,
And where thou now exacts the penalty—
Which is a pound of this poor merchant's flesh—
Thou wilt not only loose the forfeiture
25   But—touched with human gentleness and love,—
Forgive a moiety of the principal,
Glancing an eye of pity on his losses
That have of late so huddled on his back
Eno' to press a royal merchant down
30   And pluck commiseration of his state
From brassy bosoms and rough hearts of flint,
From stubborn Turks and Tartars never trained
To offices of tender courtesy.
We all expect a gentle answer, Jew.

SHYLOCK
35   I have possessed your grace of what I purpose,
And by our holy Sabbath have I sworn
To have the due and forfeit of my bond.
If you deny it, let the danger light
Upon your charter and your city's freedom.
40   You'll ask me why I rather choose to have
A weight of carrion flesh than to receive
Three thousand ducats. I'll not answer that
But say it is my humour. Is it answered?
What if my house be troubled with a rat
45   And I be pleased to give ten thousand ducats
To have it baned? What, are you answered yet?

DUKE

Make room so he can stand in front of me. Shylock, everyone thinks—and I agree—that you're just pretending to be cruel. They think that at the last second you're going to show mercy and pity, which will be more surprising than the bizarre cruelty that you seem to be showing now. And even though you're here to collect the penalty—a pound of this poor merchant's flesh—they think you'll not only let it go, but out of humanity and love you'll forgive some portion of the principal he owes you too. In doing so you'll be taking pity on him for his many recent losses, which have been large enough to send even the greatest merchant out of business, and make even the most hard-hearted Turk or Tartar feel sorry for him. What do you say? We all expect a nice answer from you, Jew.

SHYLOCK

I've told you what I intend to do, and I've sworn by the holy Sabbath to seek the penalty that is due according to our contract. If you refuse to allow me to do so, your city's charter and its freedom are endangered. You're going to ask me why I'd rather have a pound of decaying flesh than three thousand ducats. I won't answer that. Let's just say it's because I feel like it. Is that enough of an answer? What if I had a rat in my house, and I felt like paying ten thousand ducats to have it exterminated? Do you have your answer yet?

ACT FOUR

Some men there are love not a gaping pig,
Some that are mad if they behold a cat,
And others, when the bagpipe sings i' th' nose,
50 Cannot contain their urine. For affection,
Mistress of passion, sways it to the mood
Of what it likes or loathes. Now, for your answer:
As there is no firm reason to be rendered
Why he cannot abide a gaping pig;
55 Why he, a harmless necessary cat;
Why he, a woollen bagpipe, but of force
Must yield to such inevitable shame
As to offend, himself being offended—
So can I give no reason, nor I will not
60 (More than a lodged hate and a certain loathing
I bear Antonio), that I follow thus
A losing suit against him. Are you answered?

BASSANIO
This is no answer, thou unfeeling man,
To excuse the current of thy cruelty.

SHYLOCK
65 I am not bound to please thee with my answers.

BASSANIO
Do all men kill the things they do not love?

SHYLOCK
Hates any man the thing he would not kill?

BASSANIO
Every offense is not a hate at first.

SHYLOCK
What, wouldst thou have a serpent sting thee twice?

ANTONIO
70 *(to* BASSANIO*)* I pray you, think you question with the Jew?
You may as well go stand upon the beach
And bid the main flood bate his usual height.
You may as well use question with the wolf
Why he hath made the ewe bleat for the lamb.

Some men don't like roast pig, others go crazy if they see a cat, and others can't help urinating when they hear bagpipes. There's no sense trying to explain people's likes and dislikes. So, to answer your question. Just as there's no clear reason why one man doesn't want a roast pig, or why another man can't stand a harmless and useful cat, or another can't tolerate bagpipes, so I can't give a reason, and I won't give a reason (other than the simple hate and loathing I feel for Antonio) why I'm pursuing this unprofitable case against him. Does that answer your question?

BASSANIO

That's no answer, you heartless man. It doesn't excuse your cruel behavior.

SHYLOCK

I don't have to give you answers that you like.

BASSANIO

Does everyone kill what they don't love?

SHYLOCK

Does anyone hate something and not want to kill it?

BASSANIO

Disliking something isn't the same thing as hating it.

SHYLOCK

What, would you let a snake bite you twice?

ANTONIO

(to BASSANIO) Please don't bother arguing with the Jew. You might as well go stand on the beach and ask the ocean to get smaller. You might as well ask a wolf why he killed the lamb and made its mother cry.

75 You may as well forbid the mountain pines
To wag their high tops and to make no noise
When they are fretten with the gusts of heaven.
You may as well do anything most hard,
As seek to soften that—than which what's harder?—
80 His Jewish heart. Therefore I do beseech you
Make no more offers, use no farther means,
But with all brief and plain conveniency
Let me have judgment and the Jew his will.

BASSANIO
(to SHYLOCK*)* For thy three thousand ducats here is six.

SHYLOCK
85 If every ducat in six thousand ducats
Were in six parts, and every part a ducat,
I would not draw them. I would have my bond.

DUKE
How shalt thou hope for mercy, rendering none?

SHYLOCK
What judgment shall I dread, doing no wrong?
90 You have among you many a purchased slave,
Which—like your asses and your dogs and mules—
You use in abject and in slavish parts
Because you bought them. Shall I say to you,
"Let them be free! Marry them to your heirs!
95 Why sweat they under burdens? Let their beds
Be made as soft as yours and let their palates
Be seasoned with such viands"? You will answer,
"The slaves are ours." So do I answer you.
The pound of flesh which I demand of him
100 Is dearly bought. 'Tis mine and I will have it.
If you deny me, fie upon your law—
There is no force in the decrees of Venice.
I stand for judgment. Answer, shall I have it?

You might as well tell the pine trees on the mountain to stop waving their treetops when the storms blow through them. You might as well do the impossible rather than try to soften his Jewish heart. It's the hardest thing imaginable. Therefore I'm begging you, don't make any more offers, don't look for other ways to stop him. Just let me receive my punishment, and let the Jew take his penalty.

BASSANIO

(to SHYLOCK) Instead of your three thousand ducats, here are six thousand.

SHYLOCK

If you offered me six times that, I wouldn't accept it. I would choose to take my penalty.

DUKE

How can you ever hope for mercy for yourself, when you don't give any now?

SHYLOCK

Why should I be afraid of your judgment when I haven't done anything wrong? Many of you own slaves, which—like your donkeys and dogs and mules—you use to perform awful jobs just because you bought them. Should I say to you, "Set them free! Let them marry your children! Why are you making them work so hard? Let their beds be as soft as yours, and let them eat the same food as you"? No, you'd answer, "The slaves are ours." And that's just how I'm answering you. The pound of flesh that I want from him was very expensive. It's mine and I'm going to get it. If you refuse me, the laws of Venice have no validity. I await justice. So answer me. Will I get it?

ACT FOUR

DUKE
Upon my power I may dismiss this court,
105   Unless Bellario, a learnèd doctor,
Whom I have sent for to determine this,
Come here today.

SALERIO
                    My lord, here stays without
A messenger with letters from the doctor,
New come from Padua.

DUKE
110   Bring us the letter. Call the messenger.

BASSANIO
Good cheer, Antonio! What, man, courage yet!
The Jew shall have my flesh, blood, bones and all,
Ere thou shalt lose for me one drop of blood.

ANTONIO
I am a tainted wether of the flock,
115   Meetest for death. The weakest kind of fruit
Drops earliest to the ground, and so let me.
You cannot better be employed, Bassanio,
Than to live still and write mine epitaph.

Enter NERISSA, *disguised as a clerk*

DUKE
Came you from Padua, from Bellario?

NERISSA
120   From both, my lord. Bellario greets your grace.
(gives DUKE *a letter)*

SHYLOCK *sharpens a knife on the bottom of his shoe*

BASSANIO
(to SHYLOCK*)* Why dost thou whet thy knife so earnestly?

DUKE

I have the authority to dismiss this court, unless Bellario comes today. He's a legal expert I sent for to act as judge and help settle this matter.

SALERIO

My lord, a messenger is waiting outside with letters from Bellario. He's just come from Padua.

DUKE

Bring us the letters. Call the messenger in.

BASSANIO

Cheer up, Antonio! Keep up your courage, man! I'll give the Jew my flesh, blood, bones, and everything before you lose one drop of blood for me.

ANTONIO

I'm like the one sick sheep in the flock, the one who deserves to die. The weakest fruit drops to the ground first, so let me drop. Bassanio, the best thing you can do is to keep living and write an epitaph for my gravestone.

NERISSA enters, disguised as a lawyer's clerk.

DUKE

Have you come from Bellario's office in Padua?

NERISSA

Yes, my lord. Bellario sends his greetings. *(she gives the DUKE a letter)*

SHYLOCK sharpens his knife on the sole of his shoe.

BASSANIO

(to SHYLOCK) Why are you sharpening your knife so eagerly?

SHYLOCK
 To cut the forfeiture from that bankrupt there.

GRATIANO
 Not on thy sole, but on thy soul, harsh Jew,
 Thou makest thy knife keen. But no metal can—
125 No, not the hangman's axe—bear half the keenness
 Of thy sharp envy. Can no prayers pierce thee?

SHYLOCK
 No, none that thou hast wit enough to make.

GRATIANO
 O, be thou damned, inexecrable dog,
 And for thy life let justice be accused!
130 Thou almost makest me waver in my faith
 To hold opinion with Pythagoras
 That souls of animals infuse themselves
 Into the trunks of men. Thy currish spirit
 Governed a wolf who, hanged for human slaughter,
135 Even from the gallows did his fell soul fleet,
 And whilst thou layest in thy unhallowed dam
 Infused itself in thee, for thy desires
 Are wolvish, bloody, starved, and ravenous.

SHYLOCK
 Till thou canst rail the seal from off my bond,
140 Thou but offend'st thy lungs to speak so loud.
 Repair thy wit, good youth, or it will fall
 To cureless ruin. I stand here for law.

DUKE
 This letter from Bellario doth commend
 A young and learnèd doctor to our court.
145 Where is he?

NERISSA
       He attendeth here hard by
 To know your answer whether you'll admit him.

SHYLOCK

To cut my penalty from that bankrupt man over there.

GRATIANO

You're sharpening that knife not on your sole but on your soul, you cruel Jew. No metal—not even the executioner's axe—could ever be half as sharp as your hatred. Can't any prayers reach your heart?

SHYLOCK

No, none that you're smart enough to make.

GRATIANO

Oh, you're going to hell, you disgusting dog. Killing you would be justice. You almost make me forget that I'm a Christian. You make me want to agree with the philosopher Pythagoras that animal souls are reincarnated in human bodies. Your vicious dog soul used to belong to a wolf that was killed for slaughtering humans. When he died, his cruel soul passed out of his body and went into yours while you were lying in your unholy mother's womb. That's why your desires are wolfish, bloody, and ravenous.

SHYLOCK

Unless your taunts can undo the signature on my contract, you're just wearing out your lungs by speaking so loud. Be quiet, boy, or you'll lose your mind. I stand here with the law on my side.

DUKE

This letter from Bellario introduces us to a young and well-educated legal expert. Where is he?

NERISSA

He's waiting nearby to find out if you'll invite him in.

DUKE
With all my heart.—Some three or four of you
Go give him courteous conduct to this place.—
Meantime the court shall hear Bellario's letter.
(reads)

150 "Your grace shall understand that at the receipt of
your letter I am very sick, but in the instant that your
messenger came, in loving visitation was with me a
young doctor of Rome. His name is Balthazar. I
acquainted him with the cause in controversy between
155 the Jew and Antonio the merchant. We turned o'er
many books together. He is furnished with my
opinion, which—bettered with his own learning, the
greatness whereof I cannot enough commend—
comes with him at my importunity to fill up your
160 grace's request in my stead. I beseech you, let his lack
of years be no impediment to let him lack a reverend
estimation, for I never knew so young a body with so
old a head. I leave him to your gracious acceptance,
whose trial shall better publish his commendation."

Enter PORTIA *for Balthazar, disguised as a doctor of law*

165 You hear the learned Bellario, what he writes.
And here I take it is the doctor come.—
Give me your hand. Come you from old Bellario?

PORTIA
I did, my lord.

DUKE
You are welcome. Take your place.
Are you acquainted with the difference
170 That holds this present question in the court?

PORTIA
I am informèd thoroughly of the cause.
Which is the merchant here, and which the Jew?

DUKE

With all my heart.—Three or four of you go welcome him.—In the meantime, I'll read Bellario's letter out loud.

(he reads)

"I've received your letter but I'm very sick at the moment. As it happened, when your messenger came, a young lawyer from Rome was visiting me. His name is Balthazar. I told him about the case of the Jew and Antonio the merchant, and we consulted many books together. He knows my legal opinions about this matter, and he has his own expert opinions as well. I'm sending him in my place to answer your request for someone to act as judge in this matter. Please don't under-estimate him because he's so young. I never knew such a young man with such a mature head. I leave him to you. When you put him to the test, you'll see how wonderful he really is. You hear what the wise and educated Bellario writes."

PORTIA *enters disguised as Balthazar, a lawyer.*

And this is the legal professor, I take it.—Let me shake your hand. Did old Bellario send you here?

PORTIA

Yes, my lord.

DUKE

Welcome. Please have a seat. Are you familiar with the case currently before the court?

PORTIA

Yes, thoroughly. Which one is the merchant? And which one is the Jew?

DUKE
　　Antonio and old Shylock, both stand forth.

PORTIA
　　Is your name Shylock?

SHYLOCK
　　　　　　　　　Shylock is my name.

PORTIA
175　　Of a strange nature is the suit you follow,
　　Yet in such rule that the Venetian law
　　Cannot impugn you as you do proceed.—
　　(to ANTONIO*)* You stand within his danger, do you not?

ANTONIO
　　Ay, so he says.

PORTIA
　　　　　　　Do you confess the bond?

ANTONIO
180　　I do.

PORTIA
　　　　　Then must the Jew be merciful.

SHYLOCK
　　On what compulsion must I? Tell me that.

PORTIA
　　The quality of mercy is not strained.
　　It droppeth as the gentle rain from heaven
　　Upon the place beneath. It is twice blessed:
185　　It blesseth him that gives and him that takes.
　　'Tis mightiest in the mightiest. It becomes
　　The thronèd monarch better than his crown.
　　His scepter shows the force of temporal power,
　　The attribute to awe and majesty
190　　Wherein doth sit the dread and fear of kings,
　　But mercy is above this sceptered sway.
　　It is enthronèd in the hearts of kings.
　　It is an attribute to God himself.
　　And earthly power doth then show likest God's
195　　When mercy seasons justice. Therefore, Jew,

DUKE

Antonio and Shylock, both of you come forward.

PORTIA

Is your name Shylock?

SHYLOCK

Shylock is my name.

PORTIA

Your case is most unusual, though the Venetian law can't stop you from proceeding.—*(to* ANTONIO*)* He has a claim on you, correct?

ANTONIO

Yes, so he says.

PORTIA

Do you acknowledge the contract?

ANTONIO

Yes, I do.

PORTIA

Then the Jew must show you mercy.

SHYLOCK

Why do I have to do that? Tell me.

PORTIA

No one shows mercy because he has to. It just happens, the way gentle rain drops on the ground. Mercy is a double blessing. It blesses the one who gives it and the one who receives it. It's strongest in the strongest people. It looks better in a king than his own crown looks on him. The king's scepter represents his earthly power, the symbol of majesty, the focus of royal authority. But mercy is higher than the scepter. It's enthroned in the hearts of kings, a quality of God himself. Kingly power seems most like God's power when the king mixes mercy with justice. So although justice is your plea, Jew, consider this.

ACT FOUR

Though justice be thy plea, consider this—
That in the course of justice none of us
Should see salvation. We do pray for mercy,
And that same prayer doth teach us all to render
200   The deeds of mercy. I have spoke thus much
To mitigate the justice of thy plea,
Which if thou follow, this strict court of Venice
Must needs give sentence 'gainst the merchant there.

SHYLOCK
My deeds upon my head. I crave the law,
205   The penalty, and forfeit of my bond.

PORTIA
Is he not able to discharge the money?

BASSANIO
Yes, here I tender it for him in the court—
Yea, twice the sum. If that will not suffice,
I will be bound to pay it ten times o'er,
210   On forfeit of my hands, my head, my heart.
If this will not suffice, it must appear
That malice bears down truth.—
(to DUKE*)*

                    And I beseech you,
Wrest once the law to your authority.
To do a great right, do a little wrong,
And curb this cruel devil of his will.

PORTIA
215   It must not be. There is no power in Venice
Can alter a decree establishèd.
'Twill be recorded for a precedent,
And many an error by the same example
Will rush into the state. It cannot be.

SHYLOCK
220   A Daniel come to judgment, yea, a Daniel!—
O wise young judge, how I do honor thee!

Justice won't save our souls. We pray for mercy, and this same prayer teaches us to show mercy to others as well. I've told you this to make you give up this case. If you pursue it, this strict court of Venice will need to carry out the sentence against the merchant there.

SHYLOCK

I take all responsibility for my decisions. I want the law, the penalty, and the fulfillment of my contract.

PORTIA

Can't he pay back the money?

BASSANIO

Yes. I'm offering to pay it back right this moment—even twice the sum. If that's not enough, I'll sign a contract to pay ten times that much, and I'll give you my hands, my head, and my heart as security. If that's not enough, then you're just evil and malicious.—*(to the* DUKE*)* I beg you, just this once, use your authority to bend the law. Do a great right by doing a little wrong. Don't let this devil have his way.

PORTIA

That can't happen. There's no power in Venice that can change an established decree. The change will be recorded as a precedent, and many bad legal decisions will result. That can't happen.

SHYLOCK

In the Bible, as a young man, Daniel shows great wisdom while acting as judge in the case of Susanna, who was falsely accused.

A Daniel has come to judgment, yes, a Daniel!—Oh, wise young judge, I honor you!

PORTIA
>I pray you, let me look upon the bond.

SHYLOCK
>*(giving* PORTIA *a document)*
>Here 'tis, most reverend doctor, here it is.

PORTIA
>Shylock, there's thrice thy money offered thee.

SHYLOCK
225
>An oath, an oath, I have an oath in heaven.
>Shall I lay perjury upon my soul?
>No, not for Venice.

PORTIA
>   Why, this bond is forfeit!
>And lawfully by this the Jew may claim
>A pound of flesh to be by him cut off
230
>Nearest the merchant's heart.—Be merciful.
>Take thrice thy money. Bid me tear the bond.

SHYLOCK
>When it is paid according to the tenor.
>It doth appear you are a worthy judge.
>You know the law. Your exposition
235
>Hath been most sound. I charge you by the law,
>Whereof you are a well-deserving pillar,
>Proceed to judgment. By my soul I swear
>There is no power in the tongue of man
>To alter me. I stay here on my bond.

ANTONIO
240
>Most heartily I do beseech the court
>To give the judgment.

PORTIA
>   Why then, thus it is:
>You must prepare your bosom for his knife.

SHYLOCK
>O noble judge! O excellent young man!

PORTIA

Please, let me review the contract.

SHYLOCK

(he hands PORTIA *a paper)* Here it is, judge, here it is.

PORTIA

Shylock, they're offering you three times the money you lent.

SHYLOCK

But I made an oath, an oath, an oath in heaven. Should I perjure my soul by disobeying it? No, not for all of Venice.

PORTIA

The money wasn't paid back! And so the Jew may lawfully claim a pound of flesh nearest the merchant's heart, to be cut off by him.—But please have mercy. Take three times your money. Tell me to tear up this contract.

SHYLOCK

I'll tear it up when it's paid. You seem like a good judge. You know the law. Your explanation has made sense. I urge you to deliver your verdict. I swear that nothing anyone can say will change my mind. I'm sticking to the contract.

ANTONIO

I beg the court to deliver the verdict.

PORTIA

Well, then, here it is: you must prepare yourself for his knife.

SHYLOCK

Oh, good judge! Oh, you excellent young man!

PORTIA
For the intent and purpose of the law
245   Hath full relation to the penalty,
Which here appeareth due upon the bond.

SHYLOCK
'Tis very true. O wise and upright judge!
How much more elder art thou than thy looks!

PORTIA
(to **ANTONIO***)* Therefore lay bare your bosom.

SHYLOCK
Ay, his breast.
250   So says the bond. Doth it not, noble judge?
"Nearest his heart"—those are the very words.

PORTIA
It is so. Are there balance here to weigh
The flesh?

SHYLOCK
I have them ready.

PORTIA
Have by some surgeon, Shylock, on your charge,
255   To stop his wounds lest he do bleed to death.

SHYLOCK
Is it so nominated in the bond?

PORTIA
It is not so expressed, but what of that?
'Twere good you do so much for charity.

SHYLOCK
I cannot find it. 'Tis not in the bond.

PORTIA
260   *(to* **ANTONIO***)* You, merchant, have you any thing to say?

ANTONIO
But little. I am armed and well prepared.—
Give me your hand, Bassanio. Fare you well.

PORTIA

The law fully authorizes the penalty, which you have to pay according to the contract.

SHYLOCK

Very true. O wise judge! You're so much older than you look!

PORTIA

(to ANTONIO*)* So bare your chest.

SHYLOCK

Yes, his chest! That's what the contract says, doesn't it, judge? "Nearest his heart."—Those are the very words.

PORTIA

Yes. Is there a scale here to weigh the flesh?

SHYLOCK

I have it ready.

PORTIA

Pay a surgeon to stand by and bind his wounds, Shylock, so he doesn't bleed to death.

SHYLOCK

Is that called for in the contract?

PORTIA

Not explicitly, but so what? It wouldn't hurt you to be charitable.

SHYLOCK

I can't find it. It's not in the contract.

PORTIA

(to ANTONIO*)* You, merchant, do you have anything to say?

ANTONIO

Not much. I'm ready and waiting.—Give me your hand, Bassanio. Goodbye.

Grieve not that I am fall'n to this for you,
For herein Fortune shows herself more kind
265   Than is her custom. It is still her use
To let the wretched man outlive his wealth,
To view with hollow eye and wrinkled brow
An age of poverty—from which lingering penance
Of such misery doth she cut me off.
270   Commend me to your honorable wife.
Tell her the process of Antonio's end.
Say how I loved you. Speak me fair in death.
And when the tale is told, bid her be judge
Whether Bassanio had not once a love.
275   Repent but you that you shall lose your friend,
And he repents not that he pays your debt.
For if the Jew do cut but deep enough,
I'll pay it presently with all my heart.

BASSANIO
Antonio, I am married to a wife
280   Which is as dear to me as life itself.
But life itself, my wife, and all the world
Are not with me esteemed above thy life.
I would lose all—ay, sacrifice them all
Here to this devil—to deliver you.

PORTIA
285   Your wife would give you little thanks for that
If she were by to hear you make the offer.

GRATIANO
I have a wife, whom I protest I love.
I would she were in heaven, so she could
Entreat some power to change this currish Jew.

NERISSA
290   'Tis well you offer it behind her back.
The wish would make else an unquiet house.

Don't be sad that this happened because of you, because Lady Luck's been nicer to me than usual. Usually she makes the unhappy man live on after he loses his wealth, to spend his old age in poverty. But in my case she's letting me avoid that misery. Send your honorable wife my greetings, and tell her how I died and how I loved you. Speak well of me after I'm dead, and when the tale's done, ask her to judge whether Bassanio had a friend. Be sad only at the fact that you'll lose your friend—your friend doesn't regret that he paid your debt. If the Jew cuts deep enough, I'll pay it instantly with all my heart.

BASSANIO

Antonio, I married a woman as dear to me as life itself. But life itself, my wife, and the whole world aren't more valuable to me than your life is. I'd give it all up—yes, I'd sacrifice them all to this devil here—to save you.

PORTIA

Your wife wouldn't like it if she were here to hear you make that offer.

GRATIANO

I have a wife I love. I wish she were in heaven so she could appeal to some power to make this dog Jew change his mind.

NERISSA

It's nice you're offering to sacrifice her behind her back. That wish of yours could start quite an argument back at home.

SHYLOCK
These be the Christian husbands. I have a daughter.
Would any of the stock of Barabbas
Had been her husband rather than a Christian!—
295   We trifle time. I pray thee, pursue sentence.

PORTIA
A pound of that same merchant's flesh is thine.
The court awards it, and the law doth give it.

SHYLOCK
Most rightful judge!

PORTIA
And you must cut this flesh from off his breast.
300   The law allows it, and the court awards it.

SHYLOCK
Most learnèd judge, a sentence! Come, prepare.

PORTIA
Tarry a little. There is something else.
This bond doth give thee here no jot of blood.
The words expressly are "a pound of flesh."
305   Take then thy bond, take thou thy pound of flesh,
But in the cutting it if thou dost shed
One drop of Christian blood, thy lands and goods
Are by the laws of Venice confiscate
Unto the state of Venice.

GRATIANO
310   O upright judge!—Mark, Jew.—O learnèd judge!

SHYLOCK
Is that the law?

PORTIA
Thyself shalt see the act.
For as thou urgest justice, be assured
Thou shalt have justice more than thou desirest.

SHYLOCK

That's what you get for marrying Christian husbands. I have a daughter. I wish she'd married any one of Barabbas's descendants instead of a Christian!— We're wasting time. Please, deliver the sentence.

In the Bible, Barabbas is a thief who is set free at the same time that Jesus is condemned to death.

PORTIA

A pound of this merchant's flesh is yours. The court awards it and the law authorizes it.

SHYLOCK

What a righteous judge!

PORTIA

And you have to cut this flesh from his chest. The law allows it, and the court awards it.

SHYLOCK

What a wise judge! Come on, get ready.

PORTIA

But wait a moment. There's something else. This contract doesn't give you any blood at all. The words expressly specify "a pound of flesh." So take your penalty of a pound of flesh, but if you shed one drop of Christian blood when you cut it, the state of Venice will confiscate your land and property under Venetian law.

GRATIANO

Oh, what an upright judge!—Pay attention, Jew.— Oh, what a smart judge!

SHYLOCK

Is that the law?

PORTIA

You can see for yourself. You asked for justice, so rest assured you'll get more justice than you bargained for.

GRATIANO

315   O learnèd judge!—Mark, Jew, a learnèd judge!

SHYLOCK

I take this offer then: pay the bond thrice
And let the Christian go.

BASSANIO

                       Here is the money.

PORTIA

Soft!
The Jew shall have all justice. Soft, no haste.

320   He shall have nothing but the penalty.

GRATIANO

O Jew! An upright judge, a learnèd judge!

PORTIA

Therefore prepare thee to cut off the flesh.
Shed thou no blood, nor cut thou less nor more
But just a pound of flesh. If thou takest more

325   Or less than a just pound, be it but so much
As makes it light or heavy in the substance
Or the division of the twentieth part
Of one poor scruple—nay, if the scale do turn
But in the estimation of a hair,

330   Thou diest and all thy goods are confiscate.

GRATIANO

A second Daniel!—A Daniel, Jew!
Now, infidel, I have you on the hip.

PORTIA

Why doth the Jew pause? Take thy forfeiture.

SHYLOCK

Give me my principal, and let me go.

BASSANIO

335   I have it ready for thee. Here it is.

GRATIANO

Oh, what a wise judge!—Pay attention, Jew. A wise judge!

SHYLOCK

In that case I'll take their offer. Pay me three times the amount of the loan and let the Christian go.

BASSANIO

Here is the money.

PORTIA

Wait! The Jew will have justice. Wait, don't rush! He's not getting anything except the penalty.

GRATIANO

Oh, Jew, what an upright judge this is! What a wise judge!

PORTIA

So get ready to cut off the flesh. Don't shed any blood, or cut less or more than exactly a pound of flesh. If you take more or less than exactly a pound, even if it's just the tiniest fraction of an ounce—if the scale changes by even so much as a hair, you die, and all your property will be confiscated.

GRATIANO

A second Daniel!—A Daniel, Jew! I've got you now, pagan.

PORTIA

Why is the Jew waiting? Take your penalty.

SHYLOCK

Give me my money and let me go.

BASSANIO

I have it ready for you. Here it is.

PORTIA
　　He hath refused it in the open court.
　　He shall have merely justice and his bond.

GRATIANO
　　A Daniel, still say I, a second Daniel!—
　　I thank thee, Jew, for teaching me that word.

SHYLOCK
340　　Shall I not have barely my principal?

PORTIA
　　Thou shalt have nothing but the forfeiture
　　To be so taken at thy peril, Jew.

SHYLOCK
　　Why then, the devil give him good of it!
　　I'll stay no longer question.

PORTIA
　　　　　　　　　　　Tarry, Jew.
345　　The law hath yet another hold on you.
　　It is enacted in the laws of Venice,
　　If it be proved against an alien
　　That by direct or indirect attempts
　　He seek the life of any citizen,
350　　The party 'gainst the which he doth contrive
　　Shall seize one half his goods. The other half
　　Comes to the privy coffer of the state,
　　And the offender's life lies in the mercy
　　Of the Duke only 'gainst all other voice.
355　　In which predicament I say thou stand'st,
　　For it appears by manifest proceeding
　　That indirectly—and directly too—
　　Thou hast contrived against the very life
　　Of the defendant, and thou hast incurred
360　　The danger formerly by me rehearsed.
　　Down, therefore, and beg mercy of the Duke.

PORTIA

No, he refused it publicly, in open court. He will have only justice and his penalty.

GRATIANO

A Daniel, I keep saying it! A second Daniel!—Thank you, Jew, for teaching me that word.

SHYLOCK

I won't even get the original three thousand ducats back?

PORTIA

You can't have anything but the penalty, to be taken at your peril, Jew.

SHYLOCK

Well, then, I hope he chokes on it! I'm not staying here to argue anymore.

PORTIA

Wait a minute, Jew. The law has another hold on you. The laws of Venice state that if a foreign resident directly or indirectly attempts to kill any citizen, the person he tried to kill will receive one half of the foreigner's goods. The other half goes to the state. Whether the offending person lives or dies is up to the duke—there's no one else to appeal to. In your predicament you've earned that punishment, because you've clearly contrived indirectly—and directly too—to take the life of the defendant. So get down on your knees and beg mercy from the duke.

GRATIANO
    Beg that thou mayst have leave to hang thyself,
    And yet, thy wealth being forfeit to the state,
    Thou hast not left the value of a cord.
365   Therefore thou must be hanged at the state's charge.

DUKE
    That thou shalt see the difference of our spirit,
    I pardon thee thy life before thou ask it.
    For half thy wealth, it is Antonio's.
    The other half comes to the general state,
370   Which humbleness may drive unto a fine.

PORTIA
    Ay, for the state, not for Antonio.

SHYLOCK
    Nay, take my life and all. Pardon not that.
    You take my house when you do take the prop
    That doth sustain my house. You take my life
375   When you do take the means whereby I live.

PORTIA
    What mercy can you render him, Antonio?

GRATIANO
    A halter gratis, nothing else, for God's sake.

ANTONIO
    So please my lord the duke and all the court,
    To quit the fine for one half of his goods
380   I am content, so he will let me have
    The other half in use to render it
    Upon his death unto the gentleman
    That lately stole his daughter.
    Two things provided more: that for this favor
385   He presently become a Christian;
    The other, that he do record a gift
    Here in the court, of all he dies possessed,
    Unto his son Lorenzo and his daughter.

GRATIANO

Beg to be allowed to hang yourself! But if you've handed over all your wealth to the state, you don't even have enough money left to buy a rope. So you'll be hanged at the state's expense.

DUKE

I want you to see the difference between us, so I pardon you even before you ask for a pardon. Half of your wealth goes to Antonio. The other half goes to the state. However, if you show a proper humility, I may reduce this penalty to a fine.

PORTIA

Yes, the state's half can be reduced, but not Antonio's.

SHYLOCK

No, go ahead and take my life. Don't pardon that. You take my house away when you take the money I need for upkeep. You take my life when you take away my means of making a living.

PORTIA

What mercy can you show him, Antonio?

GRATIANO

A hangman's rope free of charge. Nothing else, for God's sake!

ANTONIO

If the duke and his court agree to set aside the fine for one half of his property, I'm happy, as long as he lets me have the other half in trust, to give it to the gentleman who recently stole his daughter. I only ask two more things. First, Shylock must immediately become a Christian. Second, he must make a will here in this court that leaves all his property to his son-in-law Lorenzo and his daughter when he dies.

DUKE
390   He shall do this, or else I do recant
      The pardon that I late pronouncèd here.

PORTIA
      Art thou contented, Jew? What dost thou say?

SHYLOCK
      I am content.

PORTIA
      (to NERISSA*)*
                Clerk, draw a deed of gift.

SHYLOCK
      I pray you, give me leave to go from hence.
      I am not well. Send the deed after me,
      And I will sign it.

DUKE
                Get thee gone, but do it.

GRATIANO
      (to SHYLOCK*)*
395   In christening shalt thou have two godfathers.
      Had I been judge, thou shouldst have had ten more—
      To bring thee to the gallows, not to the font.

                              Exit SHYLOCK

DUKE
      (to PORTIA*)* Sir, I entreat you home with me to dinner.

PORTIA
      I humbly do desire your grace of pardon.
400   I must away this night toward Padua,
      And it is meet I presently set forth.

DUKE
      I am sorry that your leisure serves you not.—
      Antonio, gratify this gentleman,
      For in my mind you are much bound to him.

                       Exit DUKE *and his train*

DUKE

He must do this, or I'll recant the pardon I just delivered.

PORTIA

Are you satisfied, Jew? What do you say?

SHYLOCK

I'm satisfied.

PORTIA

(to NERISSA) Clerk, draw up a document to make his gift official.

SHYLOCK

Please let me go. I'm not well. Send the deed after me and I'll sign it.

DUKE

Go, but sign the deed.

GRATIANO

(to SHYLOCK) When you're baptized a Christian, you'll have two godfathers. If I'd been the judge, you would've had ten more—twelve jurors to sentence you to death rather than baptism.

SHYLOCK *exits.*

DUKE

(to PORTIA) Sir, please come home with me to dinner.

PORTIA

I'm very sorry, sir, but I have to go to Padua tonight. I should really leave right away.

DUKE

I'm sorry you don't have time.—Antonio, give this gentleman a reward. In my opinion, you owe him a lot.

The DUKE and his entourage exit.

BASSANIO

405   *(to* PORTIA*)* Most worthy gentleman, I and my friend
        Have by your wisdom been this day acquitted
        Of grievous penalties, in lieu whereof
        Three thousand ducats due unto the Jew
        We freely cope your courteous pains withal.

ANTONIO

410   And stand indebted, over and above,
        In love and service to you evermore.

PORTIA

        He is well paid that is well satisfied.
        And I, delivering you, am satisfied,
        And therein do account myself well paid.

415   My mind was never yet more mercenary.
        I pray you, know me when we meet again.
        I wish you well, and so I take my leave.

BASSANIO

        Dear sir, of force I must attempt you further.
        Take some remembrance of us as a tribute,

420   Not as a fee. Grant me two things, I pray you:
        Not to deny me, and to pardon me.

PORTIA

        You press me far and therefore I will yield.
        (to ANTONIO*)*
        Give me your gloves. I'll wear them for your sake.
        (to BASSANIO*)*
        And for your love, I'll take this ring from you.

425   Do not draw back your hand. I'll take no more,
        And you in love shall not deny me this.

BASSANIO

        This ring, good sir—alas, it is a trifle.
        I will not shame myself to give you this.

PORTIA

        I will have nothing else but only this.

430   And now methinks I have a mind to it.

BASSANIO

> *(to* PORTIA*)* Sir, thanks to you my friend and I have been freed from paying some awful penalties today. Instead of giving the Jew the three thousand ducats he's owed, we give it to you in gratitude for your kind efforts.

ANTONIO

> And even then we're still indebted to you. We owe you love and service forever.

PORTIA

> Being satisfied with a job well done is payment enough. In saving you I consider myself well paid. My thoughts were never on money. I hope you'll recognize me when we meet again. I wish you well. Now, I've got to go.

BASSANIO

> Sir, I really feel the need to give you something. Take some memento from us as a token of our gratitude, not as a fee. Please do two favors for me. First, don't refuse me, and second, excuse me for insisting.

PORTIA

> Since you keep insisting, I'll do as you say. *(to* ANTONIO*)* Give me your gloves. I'll wear them for your sake. *(to* BASSANIO*)* And as a souvenir of your appreciation, I'll take this ring from you. Don't pull your hand back. I won't take anything more than this, and you can't refuse me this.

BASSANIO

> This ring, sir—oh no, it's nothing. I'd be ashamed to give you this.

PORTIA

> I don't want anything but that. Now that I think about it, I really want it.

BASSANIO
There's more depends on this than on the value.
The dearest ring in Venice will I give you,
And find it out by proclamation.
Only for this, I pray you, pardon me.

PORTIA
435   I see, sir, you are liberal in offers.
You taught me first to beg, and now methinks
You teach me how a beggar should be answered.

BASSANIO
Good sir, this ring was given me by my wife.
And when she put it on, she made me vow
440   That I should neither sell nor give nor lose it.

PORTIA
That 'scuse serves many men to save their gifts.
An if your wife be not a madwoman,
And know how well I have deserved the ring,
She would not hold out enemy forever
445   For giving it to me. Well, peace be with you.
Exeunt PORTIA *and* NERISSA

ANTONIO
My Lord Bassanio, let him have the ring.
Let his deservings and my love withal
Be valued against your wife's commandment.

BASSANIO
(*giving* GRATIANO *the ring*)
Go, Gratiano, run and overtake him.
450   Give him the ring and bring him, if thou canst,
Unto Antonio's house. Away, make haste.
Exit GRATIANO

Come, you and I will thither presently.
And in the morning early will we both
Fly toward Belmont. Come, Antonio.

Exeunt

BASSANIO

There's more to this ring than its cash value. I'll give you the most expensive ring in Venice, and I'll make a public announcement to help me find it. But as for this ring, please excuse me.

PORTIA

I see you like to make big offers, sir. First you taught me how to beg, and now I think you're teaching me how a beggar should be answered.

BASSANIO

Good sir, this ring was given to me by my wife. When she put it on my finger, she made me swear never to sell it, give it away, or lose it.

PORTIA

Many men use that excuse to avoid giving gifts. If your wife's not a madwoman, and you tell her how much I deserve this ring, she won't stay angry at you forever if you give it to me. Well, anyway, goodbye.

PORTIA and NERISSA exit.

ANTONIO

Bassanio, let him have the ring. Consider how much he deserves it, and weigh that, along with my friendship, against your wife's order.

BASSANIO

(he gives GRATIANO the ring) Go, Gratiano, run and catch up with him. Give him the ring, and take him to Antonio's house if you can. Go quickly.

GRATIANO exits.

Come on, you and I will go soon. Early in the morning we'll both rush to Belmont. Come on, Antonio.

They exit.

ACT FOUR

—∾—

ACT FOUR, Scene 2

Enter PORTIA *and* NERISSA, *both disguised*

PORTIA
Inquire the Jew's house out. Give him this deed,
And let him sign it. We'll away tonight,
And be a day before our husbands home.
This deed will be well welcome to Lorenzo.

Enter GRATIANO

GRATIANO
(giving PORTIA BASSANIO's *ring)*
5   Fair sir, you are well o'erta'en.
My Lord Bassanio upon more advice
Hath sent you here this ring, and doth entreat
Your company at dinner.

PORTIA
                                              That cannot be.
His ring I do accept most thankfully.
10   And so I pray you tell him. Furthermore,
I pray you show my youth old Shylock's house.

GRATIANO
That will I do.

NERISSA
(to PORTIA)
                              Sir, I would speak with you.
(aside to PORTIA)
I'll see if I can get my husband's ring,
Which I did make him swear to keep for ever.

PORTIA
(aside to NERISSA)
15   Thou mayst, I warrant. We shall have old swearing
That they did give the rings away to men.
But we'll outface them, and outswear them too.—

ACT FOUR, Scene 2

PORTIA *and* NERISSA *enter, both still in disguise.*

PORTIA

Find out where the Jew's house is. Give him this deed and have him sign it. We'll leave tonight and be home a day before our husbands get back. Lorenzo will be happy with what we've done.

GRATIANO *enters.*

GRATIANO

(he gives PORTIA BASSANIO's *ring)* Sir, you're lucky I caught up with you. Bassanio thought about it some more and sent this ring to you. He would like to invite you to dinner.

PORTIA

I can't have dinner with him. Please tell him I accept his ring with thanks. And could you please take my servant to old Shylock's house?

GRATIANO

I'll do that.

NERISSA

(to PORTIA*)* Sir, may I speak with you? *(speaking so that only* PORTIA*can hear)* I'll see if I can get my husband's ring, which I made him swear to keep forever.

PORTIA

(to NERISSA*)* I bet you'll be able to. They'll swear they gave the rings to men. But we'll deny it and outswear them too.—

Away, make haste. Thou know'st where I will tarry.

Exit PORTIA

NERISSA
(to GRATIANO*)*
Come, good sir. Will you show me to this house?

Exeunt

Go, hurry. You know where I'll be waiting.

She exits.

NERISSA

(to GRATIANO*)* Sir, will you show me to Shylock's house now?

They exit.

ACT FIVE

Scene 1

Enter LORENZO *and* JESSICA

LORENZO
>The moon shines bright. In such a night as this,
>When the sweet wind did gently kiss the trees
>And they did make no noise, in such a night
>Troilus methinks mounted the Trojan walls
>5   And sighed his soul toward the Grecian tents
>Where Cressid lay that night.

JESSICA
>   In such a night
>Did Thisbe fearfully o'ertrip the dew
>And saw the lion's shadow ere himself
>And ran dismayed away.

LORENZO
>   In such a night
>10   Stood Dido with a willow in her hand
>Upon the wild sea banks, and waft her love
>To come again to Carthage.

JESSICA
>   In such a night
>Medea gathered the enchanted herbs
>That did renew old Æson.

ACT FIVE

Scene 1

LORENZO *and* JESSICA *enter.*

LORENZO

> The moon's bright tonight. I think that on a night like this, when the wind blew the trees so gently that they didn't make a sound, Troilus climbed up onto the walls of Troy and sighed for Cressida in the Greek camp.

Troilus was the son of King Priam of Troy. His lover, Cressida, was sent to the Greek camp, where she betrayed him.

JESSICA

Thisbe had agreed to meet her lover Pyramus, but was frightened away by a lion. Pyramus killed himself because he thought the lion had eaten her, and Thisbe killed herself when she found Pyramus dead.

> On a night like this, Thisbe saw the lion's shadow and ran away in fear.

LORENZO

Dido, the queen of Carthage, was abandoned by her lover Aeneas.

> On a night like this, Dido stood holding a willow branch on the seashore, begging her lover to come back to her in Carthage.

JESSICA

Medea used her magic to help her lover, Jason's father. Later, Jason betrayed her, and she murdered their children in revenge.

> On a night like this, Medea gathered magic herbs to rejuvenate old Aeson.

LORENZO
                                    In such a night
Did Jessica steal from the wealthy Jew,
And with an unthrift love did run from Venice
As far as Belmont.

JESSICA
                        In such a night
Did young Lorenzo swear he loved her well,
Stealing her soul with many vows of faith,
And ne'er a true one.

LORENZO
                                    In such a night
Did pretty Jessica, like a little shrew,
Slander her love, and he forgave it her.

JESSICA
I would outnight you, did nobody come.
But, hark, I hear the footing of a man.

Enter STEPHANO, *a messenger*

LORENZO
Who comes so fast in silence of the night?

STEPHANO
A friend.

LORENZO
A friend? What friend? Your name, I pray you, friend?

STEPHANO
Stephano is my name, and I bring word
My mistress will before the break of day
Be here at Belmont. She doth stray about
By holy crosses, where she kneels and prays
For happy wedlock hours.

LORENZO
                                    Who comes with her?

LORENZO

On a night like this, Jessica ran away from the wealthy Jew and stole his money. She ran away from Venice all the way to Belmont with her spendthrift lover.

JESSICA

On a night like this, young Lorenzo swore he loved her very much, stealing her heart with vows of love, but not one vow was true.

LORENZO

On a night like this, pretty Jessica, in a bad mood, said outrageously wrong things about her lover, and he forgave her.

JESSICA

I'd get the better of you in this storytelling game, but somebody's coming. I hear his footsteps.

STEPHANO, *a messenger, enters.*

LORENZO

Who are you, coming so fast in this quiet night?

STEPHANO

A friend.

LORENZO

A friend? What friend? What's your name, please, friend?

STEPHANO

My name's Stephano, and I've come to tell you my mistress will arrive here at Belmont before sunrise. She's still at the monastery, kneeling and praying for a happy marriage.

LORENZO

Who's coming with her?

STEPHANO
None but a holy hermit and her maid.
I pray you, is my master yet returned?

LORENZO
35 He is not, nor we have not heard from him.—
But go we in, I pray thee, Jessica,
And ceremoniously let us prepare
Some welcome for the mistress of the house.

Enter LAUNCELOT *the clown*

LAUNCELOT
Sola, sola! Wo, ha, ho! Sola, sola!

LORENZO
40 Who calls?

LAUNCELOT
Sola! Did you see Master Lorenzo? Master Lorenzo, sola, sola!

LORENZO
Leave holloaing, man. Here.

LAUNCELOT
Sola! Where, where?

LORENZO
Here.

LAUNCELOT
45 Tell him there's a post come from my master with his horn
full of good news. My master will be here ere morning.

Exit LAUNCELOT

LORENZO
Sweet soul, let's in, and there expect their coming.
And yet no matter. Why should we go in?—
My friend Stephano, signify, I pray you,
50 Within the house, your mistress is at hand.
And bring your music forth into the air.

Exit STEPHANO

STEPHANO

No one except her maid and a holy hermit. Has my master returned yet?

LORENZO

No, he hasn't, and we haven't heard from him.—But let's go in, Jessica. We'll get ready to welcome the mistress of the house back home.

LAUNCELOT enters.

LAUNCELOT

Hey, hey! Hey! Yoo-hoo!

LORENZO

Who's shouting?

LAUNCELOT

Hey! Have you seen Master Lorenzo! Master Lorenzo, hey! Hey!

LORENZO

Stop hollering, man! I'm here.

LAUNCELOT

Hey! Where, where?

LORENZO

Here.

LAUNCELOT

Tell him a messenger has arrived from my master with good news. My master will be here in the morning.

LAUNCELOT exits.

LORENZO

My dear, let's go inside and wait for them to arrive. But I guess it doesn't matter. Why should we go in?— Stephano, tell the household staff that your mistress is about to arrive, and bring some musicians outside here.

STEPHANO exits.

ACT FIVE

How sweet the moonlight sleeps upon this bank!
Here will we sit and let the sounds of music
Creep in our ears. Soft stillness and the night
55   Become the touches of sweet harmony.
Sit, Jessica. Look how the floor of heaven
Is thick inlaid with patens of bright gold.
There's not the smallest orb which thou behold'st
But in his motion like an angel sings,
60   Still choiring to the young-eyed cherubins.
Such harmony is in immortal souls,
But whilst this muddy vesture of decay
Doth grossly close it in, we cannot hear it.

Enter musicians

Come ho, and wake Diana with a hymn!
65   With sweetest touches pierce your mistress' ear,
And draw her home with music.

Play music

JESSICA
I am never merry when I hear sweet music.
LORENZO
The reason is your spirits are attentive.
For do but note a wild and wanton herd,
70   Or race of youthful and unhandled colts,
Fetching mad bounds, bellowing and neighing loud,
Which is the hot condition of their blood—
If they but hear perchance a trumpet sound,
Or any air of music touch their ears,
75   You shall perceive them make a mutual stand,
Their savage eyes turned to a modest gaze
By the sweet power of music.

How beautiful the moonlight's shining on this bank! Let's sit here and let the music fill our ears. Stillness and nighttime are perfect for beautiful music. Sit down, Jessica. Look at the stars, see how the floor of heaven is inlaid with small disks of bright gold. Stars and planets move in such perfect harmony that some believe you can hear music in their movement. If you believe this, even the smallest star sings like an angel in its motion. Souls have that same kind of harmony. But because we're here on earth in our earthly bodies, we can't hear it.

Musicians enter.

Wake up the moon goddess with a hymn! Get her attention and draw her home with music.

Music plays.

JESSICA
I'm never in the mood to laugh when I hear sweet music.

LORENZO
That's because your soul is paying attention to the music. Take a wild herd of animals, or young untrained colts, leaping around like crazy, roaring and neighing loudly, which they have to do because it's in their blood—but if they happen to hear a trumpet, or any kind of music, they all stand still. Sweet music makes their wild eyes peaceful. That's why the poet

ACT FIVE

Therefore the poet

Did feign that Orpheus drew trees, stones, and floods
Since naught so stockish, hard, and full of rage,

80 But music for the time doth change his nature.
The man that hath no music in himself,
Nor is not moved with concord of sweet sounds,
Is fit for treasons, stratagems, and spoils.
The motions of his spirit are dull as night,

85 And his affections dark as Erebus.
Let no such man be trusted. Mark the music.

Enter PORTIA *and* NERISSA

PORTIA
That light we see is burning in my hall.
How far that little candle throws his beams!
So shines a good deed in a naughty world.

NERISSA
90 When the moon shone we did not see the candle.

PORTIA
So doth the greater glory dim the less.
A substitute shines brightly as a king
Until a king be by, and then his state
Empties itself, as doth an inland brook

95 Into the main of waters. Music, hark.

NERISSA
It is your music, madam, of the house.

PORTIA
Nothing is good, I see, without respect.
Methinks it sounds much sweeter than by day.

NERISSA
Silence bestows that virtue on it, madam.

PORTIA
100 The crow doth sing as sweetly as the lark

Ovid wrote that the great musician Orpheus could make trees, stones, and rivers come to him by playing music. There's nothing in the world that can resist music. The man who can't be moved by the harmonious melodies is fit only for treason, violence, and pillage. His soul is as dull as night and dark as the underworld. Nobody like that should be trusted. Pay attention to the music.

PORTIA *and* NERISSA *enter.*

PORTIA

That light we see is coming from my hall. Look how far that little candle sends its light! That's the way a good deed shines in a naughty world.

NERISSA

While the moon was shining we didn't even notice the candle.

PORTIA

Well, brighter lights always dim the smaller ones. A governor shines as brightly as a king until a king is near by, and the governor suddenly looks like a nobody. Music, listen!

NERISSA

It's your music, madam, from your house.

PORTIA

Now I see that you can't call anything good except in the right context. I think that music sounds much better at night than it does during the day.

NERISSA

The night's silence makes it sound better.

PORTIA

The crow sings as well as the lark when no one's listening. If the nightingale sang during the day, when

ACT FIVE

When neither is attended, and I think
The nightingale, if she should sing by day
When every goose is cackling, would be thought
No better a musician than the wren.
105 How many things by season seasoned are
To their right praise and true perfection!
Peace! How the moon sleeps with Endymion
And would not be awaked.

Music ceases

LORENZO
                           That is the voice,
Or I am much deceived, of Portia.

PORTIA
110 He knows me as the blind man knows the cuckoo—
By the bad voice.

LORENZO
Dear lady, welcome home.

PORTIA
We have been praying for our husbands' welfare,
Which speed, we hope, the better for our words.
115 Are they returned?

LORENZO
                Madam, they are not yet,
But there is come a messenger before
To signify their coming.

PORTIA
                   Go in, Nerissa.
Give order to my servants that they take
No note at all of our being absent hence.—
120 Nor you, Lorenzo.—Jessica, nor you.

A tucket sounds

every goose is honking, nobody would think it sang any better than a wren. How many things in life seem good to us because of when they happen! Quiet now! Look how the moon seems to be sleeping with its lover and can't be awoken!

Music ceases.

LORENZO

If I'm not mistaken, that's Portia's voice.

PORTIA

He recognizes me like a blind man recognizes a cuckoo—by its bad voice.

LORENZO

Dear lady, welcome home.

PORTIA

We've been praying for our husbands' welfare. We hope they're better off because of our prayers. Have they come back?

LORENZO

No, ma'am, they haven't. But a messenger came ahead to tell us they were on their way.

PORTIA

Go inside, Nerissa. Tell my servants not to mention that we were gone. You must not, either, Lorenzo—or you, Jessica.

A trumpet sounds.

ACT FIVE

LORENZO
> Your husband is at hand. I hear his trumpet.
> We are no tell-tales, madam. Fear you not.

PORTIA
> This night methinks is but the daylight sick.
> It looks a little paler. 'Tis a day
125   Such as the day is when the sun is hid.

Enter BASSANIO, ANTONIO, GRATIANO, *and their followers*
GRATIANO *and* NERISSA *move aside and talk*

BASSANIO
> *(to* PORTIA*)* We should hold day with the Antipodes,
> If you would walk in absence of the sun.

PORTIA
> Let me give light, but let me not be light.
> For a light wife doth make a heavy husband,
130   And never be Bassanio so for me.
> But God sort all! You are welcome home, my lord.

BASSANIO
> I thank you, madam. Give welcome to my friend.
> This is the man, this is Antonio,
> To whom I am so infinitely bound.

PORTIA
135   You should in all sense be much bound to him.
> For as I hear he was much bound for you.

ANTONIO
> No more than I am well acquitted of.

PORTIA
> Sir, you are very welcome to our house.
> It must appear in other ways than words,
140   Therefore I scant this breathing courtesy.

LORENZO

Your husband's near. I hear his trumpet. We're not tattle-tales, madam, don't worry.

PORTIA

I think this night is just like sick daylight. It only looks a little paler. It looks like a day when the sun is hidden.

BASSANIO, ANTONIO, GRATIANO, and their followers enter. GRATIANO and NERISSA move aside and talk.

BASSANIO

(to PORTIA) If you walked outside at night, it would be daylight here at the same time as on the other side of the world.

PORTIA

"Light" could mean having loose morals.

I'll give light to men, but I'll never be light or unchaste. An unfaithful wife makes a husband worry, and I'll never let Bassanio worry if I can help it. I hope God figures it all out! Welcome home, my husband.

BASSANIO

Thank you, darling. I'd like to introduce you to my friend. This is Antonio, my dearest friend. We are closely tied.

PORTIA

You should be tied to him, since he tied himself up so much for you.

ANTONIO

But I've been paid back well.

PORTIA

Sir, welcome to our house. But action speaks louder than words, so I'll cut short these polite words.

GRATIANO
    (to NERISSA*)* By yonder moon I swear you do me wrong.
    In faith, I gave it to the judge's clerk.
    Would he were gelt that had it, for my part,
    Since you do take it, love, so much at heart.

PORTIA
145   A quarrel, ho, already? What's the matter?

GRATIANO
    About a hoop of gold, a paltry ring
    That she did give me, whose posy was
    For all the world like cutler's poetry
    Upon a knife, "Love me and leave me not."

NERISSA
150   What talk you of the posy or the value?
    You swore to me when I did give it you
    That you would wear it till your hour of death,
    And that it should lie with you in your grave.
    Though not for me, yet for your vehement oaths,
155   You should have been respective and have kept it.
    Gave it a judge's clerk! No, God's my judge.
    The clerk will ne'er wear hair on 's face that had it.

GRATIANO
    He will, an if he live to be a man.

NERISSA
    Ay, if a woman live to be a man.

GRATIANO
160   Now, by this hand, I gave it to a youth,
    A kind of boy, a little scrubbèd boy
    No higher than thyself, the judge's clerk,
    A prating boy that begged it as a fee.
    I could not for my heart deny it him.

PORTIA
165   You were to blame, I must be plain with you,
    To part so slightly with your wife's first gift,
    A thing stuck on with oaths upon your finger
    And so riveted with faith unto your flesh.

GRATIANO

(to NERISSA*)* I swear by that moon over there that you're doing me wrong! I'm telling the truth! I gave it to the judge's clerk. I wish the guy I gave it to had been castrated, since you're getting so upset about it.

PORTIA

What, an argument already? What's the matter?

GRATIANO

We're arguing about a hoop of gold, a cheap little ring she gave me, that had a little inscription on it, nothing more than a knife-maker's attempt at poetry. It said, "Love me and don't leave me."

NERISSA

How can you talk about the quality of the poem or the value of the ring? You swore to me when I gave it to you that you would wear it till you died, and that it would be buried with you. If you didn't want to take care of it for my sake, you should have just because you made so many vows that you'd take care of it. And now you claim you gave it to a judge's clerk! No, I swear to God that clerk will never grow a beard on his face.

GRATIANO

He will if he lives long enough to become a man.

NERISSA

Yes, if a woman grows up to be a man.

GRATIANO

I swear I gave it to a youth, a kind of boy, a little stunted boy, no taller than yourself. He was the judge's clerk, a chatty boy who wanted it as a fee. I didn't have the heart to say no to him.

PORTIA

I have to be honest with you. You were wrong to give away your wife's first gift so thoughtlessly, a thing you swore to keep on your finger and bound faithfully to your body.

I gave my love a ring and made him swear
170 Never to part with it. And here he stands.
I dare be sworn for him he would not leave it
Nor pluck it from his finger for the wealth
That the world masters. Now in faith, Gratiano,
You give your wife too unkind a cause of grief.
175 An 'twere to me, I should be mad at it.

BASSANIO
(aside) Why, I were best to cut my left hand off
And swear I lost the ring defending it.

GRATIANO
My Lord Bassanio gave his ring away
Unto the judge that begged it and indeed
180 Deserved it too. And then the boy, his clerk,
That took some pains in writing, he begged mine.
And neither man nor master would take aught
But the two rings.

PORTIA
What ring gave you my lord?
Not that, I hope, which you received of me.

BASSANIO
185 If I could add a lie unto a fault
I would deny it. but you see my finger
Hath not the ring upon it. It is gone.

PORTIA
Even so void is your false heart of truth.
By heaven, I will ne'er come in your bed
190 Until I see the ring.

NERISSA
(to GRATIANO*)*
Nor I in yours
190 Till I again see mine.

I gave my lover a ring and made him swear never to lose it or give it away. And here he is. I'd swear he wouldn't leave it behind, or even take it off his finger, for all the money in the world. To tell the truth, Gratiano, you're giving your wife a valid reason to get upset. If it were me, I'd be very upset too.

BASSANIO

(to himself) Maybe I should cut off my left hand and swear I lost the ring defending it.

GRATIANO

Bassanio gave his ring to the judge who asked for it, and deserved it too. And then his clerk, who went to a lot of trouble with the writing, begged for mine. Neither of them would take anything but the two rings.

PORTIA

Which ring did you give away, my lord? Not the one I gave you, I hope.

BASSANIO

If I could make things better by lying, I'd deny it. But you see my finger doesn't have the ring on it. It's gone.

PORTIA

Just as there's no ring on your finger, there's no truth in your heart. I swear I'll never get into your bed until I see the ring again!

NERISSA

(to GRATIANO*)* Me neither, until I see mine again!

BASSANIO

Sweet Portia,

If you did know to whom I gave the ring,
If you did know for whom I gave the ring,
And would conceive for what I gave the ring,
And how unwillingly I left the ring
195   When naught would be accepted but the ring,
You would abate the strength of your displeasure.

PORTIA

If you had known the virtue of the ring,
Or half her worthiness that gave the ring,
Or your own honor to contain the ring,
200   You would not then have parted with the ring.
What man is there so much unreasonable,
If you had pleased to have defended it
With any terms of zeal, wanted the modesty
To urge the thing held as a ceremony?
205   Nerissa teaches me what to believe.
I'll die for 't but some woman had the ring.

BASSANIO

No, by my honor, madam, by my soul,
No woman had it but a civil doctor,
Which did refuse three thousand ducats of me
210   And begged the ring, the which I did deny him
And suffered him to go displeased away—
Even he that did uphold the very life
Of my dear friend. What should I say, sweet lady?
I was enforced to send it after him.
215   I was beset with shame and courtesy.
My honor would not let ingratitude
So much besmear it. Pardon me, good lady,
For by these blessèd candles of the night,
Had you been there I think you would have begged
220   The ring of me to give the worthy doctor.

BASSANIO

My dear Portia, if you knew who I gave the ring to, for whose sake I gave the ring to him, why I gave it to him, and how unwilling I was to leave it when he wouldn't accept anything but the ring, you wouldn't be so angry.

PORTIA

If you'd known how much that ring meant, how much the woman who gave it to you is worth, or how much your honor depended on your keeping the ring, you wouldn't have let it go. Who would be so unreasonable as to insist on taking the ring if you'd defended it with any kind of zeal? Who would have had so little self-restraint that they'd insist on getting a ring with ceremonial value? Nerissa's got the right idea. I'll bet my life you gave some woman the ring!

BASSANIO

No, I swear, madam. No woman got it from me, but an expert in civil law who refused three thousand ducats but asked instead for the ring, which I denied him. I watched him leave looking discontented, even though he had saved the life of my good friend. What could I say, my dear? I had to send it to him. I was ashamed and wanted to show my good manners. I just couldn't dishonor myself by acting ungrateful to him. Please forgive me, good lady. If you'd been there, I think you would have begged me to give him the ring.

PORTIA
Let not that doctor e'er come near my house!
Since he hath got the jewel that I loved,
And that which you did swear to keep for me,
I will become as liberal as you.
225 I'll not deny him anything I have,
No, not my body, nor my husband's bed.
Know him I shall, I am well sure of it.
Lie not a night from home. Watch me like Argus.
If you do not, if I be left alone,
230 Now, by mine honor—which is yet mine own—
I'll have that doctor for my bedfellow.

NERISSA
(to GRATIANO) And I his clerk. Therefore be well advised
How you do leave me to mine own protection.

GRATIANO
Well, do you so, let not me take him then.
235 For if I do I'll mar the young clerk's pen.

ANTONIO
I am th' unhappy subject of these quarrels.

PORTIA
Sir, grieve not you. You are welcome notwithstanding.

BASSANIO
Portia, forgive me this enforcèd wrong,
And in the hearing of these many friends
240 I swear to thee, even by thine own fair eyes
Wherein I see myself—

PORTIA
                                 Mark you but that!
In both my eyes he doubly sees himself—
In each eye, one. Swear by your double self,
And there's an oath of credit!

PORTIA

Don't let that lawyer ever come near my house! Since he has the jewel I loved, which you swore you'd keep forever, I'll be as generous as you were to him. I won't deny him anything of mine, including my own body and my husband's bed. I'll recognize him all right, I'm sure of it. So don't spend one night away from this house. Watch me like a hawk. If you don't, if I'm left alone, I swear I'll have that legal expert as my bedfellow.

NERISSA

(to GRATIANO*)* And I'll have his clerk as mine. So be careful when you leave me to my own devices.

GRATIANO

Well, go ahead. But don't let me catch him, because if I do I'll break that clerk's pen.

ANTONIO

All these quarrels are about me.

PORTIA

Don't be upset. You're welcome in our home in spite of everything that's going on.

BASSANIO

Portia, forgive me for this mistake that I had to make. All these friends are my witnesses, so I swear to you, I swear by your beautiful eyes, in which I see myself reflected—

PORTIA

Did you hear that! He sees himself in my two eyes, so there's two of him. He should swear by his two-faced self, and that's an oath I'll believe!

ACT FIVE

BASSANIO

                                        Nay, but hear me.

245   Pardon this fault, and by my soul I swear
        I never more will break an oath with thee.

ANTONIO

        I once did lend my body for his wealth,
        Which but for him that had your husband's ring
        Had quite miscarried. I dare be bound again,
250   My soul upon the forfeit, that your lord
        Will never more break faith advisedly.

PORTIA

        (giving ANTONIO *a ring)*
        Then you shall be his surety. Give him this,
        And bid him keep it better than the other.

ANTONIO

        (giving BASSANIO PORTIA'S *ring)*
        Here, Lord Bassanio. Swear to keep this ring.

BASSANIO

255   By heaven, it is the same I gave the doctor!

PORTIA

        I had it of him. Pardon me, Bassanio,
        For by this ring, the doctor lay with me.

NERISSA

        (taking out a ring)
        And pardon me, my gentle Gratiano,
        For that same scrubbèd boy, the doctor's clerk,
260   In lieu of this, last night did lie with me.

GRATIANO

        Why, this is like the mending of highways
        In summer where the ways are fair enough!
        What, are we cuckolds ere we have deserved it?

BASSANIO

> No, just listen to me. If you forgive my mistake, I swear I'll never break an oath with you again.

ANTONIO

> I lent my body once to make him rich. If it hadn't been for the gentleman who now owns your husband's ring, my body would've been lost. I'd be the guarantee again, promising my soul this time as penalty, if your husband ever breaks a vow again knowingly.

PORTIA

> *(she gives* ANTONIO *a ring)* Then you'll be my guarantee. Give him this. And tell him to hold on to it better than the other one.

ANTONIO

> *(he gives* BASSANIO PORTIA*'s ring)* Here, Bassanio, swear that you'll keep this ring.

BASSANIO

> My God, it's the same one I gave the judge!

PORTIA

> I got it from him. I'm sorry, Bassanio, but the legal expert slept with me in exchange for this ring.

NERISSA

> *(she takes out a ring)* And I'm sorry too, Gratiano, but that stunted lawyer's clerk slept with me last night in exchange for this ring.

GRATIANO

> This is like fixing roads in the summer when they don't need to be fixed! What, did you cheat on us before we deserved it?

PORTIA
Speak not so grossly.—You are all amazed.
(takes out a letter)
265   Here is a letter. Read it at your leisure.
It comes from Padua, from Bellario.
There you shall find that Portia was the doctor,
Nerissa there her clerk. Lorenzo here
Shall witness I set forth as soon as you,
270   And even but now returned. I have not yet
Entered my house.—Antonio, you are welcome.
And I have better news in store for you
Than you expect.
(gives ANTONIO *another letter)*
                    Unseal this letter soon.
There you shall find three of your argosies
275   Are richly come to harbor suddenly.
You shall not know by what strange accident
I chancèd on this letter.

ANTONIO
I am dumb.

BASSANIO
(to PORTIA*)* Were you the doctor and I knew you not?

GRATIANO
280   *(to* NERISSA*)* Were you the clerk that is to make me
cuckold?

NERISSA
Ay, but the clerk that never means to do it
Unless he live until he be a man.

BASSANIO
(to PORTIA*)* Sweet doctor, you shall be my bedfellow.
285   When I am absent then lie with my wife.

ANTONIO
Sweet lady, you have given me life and living.
For here I read for certain that my ships
Are safely come to road.

PORTIA

Don't be crass.—You all look confused. *(she takes out a letter)* Here's a letter. Read it at your leisure. It comes from Padua, from Bellario. You'll find out that Portia was the lawyer, and Nerissa was her clerk. Lorenzo here will testify that I left the house right when you did, and just returned. I haven't yet entered my house.—Antonio, welcome. I have better news than you expect in store for you. *(she gives* ANTONIO *another letter)* Open this letter. You'll find out that three of your ships have suddenly arrived in the harbor loaded with a great deal of wealth. You'll never guess what a strange coincidence it was that I came across this letter.

ANTONIO

I'm speechless.

BASSANIO

(to PORTIA*)* You were the doctor, and I didn't even recognize you?

GRATIANO

(to NERISSA*)* Were you the clerk with whom my wife's going to cheat on me?

NERISSA

Yes, but the clerk will never do it, unless he grows up to be a man.

BASSANIO

(to PORTIA*)* My sweet lawyer, you'll be my bedfellow. When I'm not there, you can sleep with my wife.

ANTONIO

Madam, you've given me life and given me a living too. I've read in this letter that my ships have safely come to harbor.

ACT FIVE

PORTIA
How now, Lorenzo?
290   My clerk hath some good comforts too for you.

NERISSA
Ay, and I'll give them him without a fee.
(gives LORENZO *a document)*
There do I give to you and Jessica,
From the rich Jew, a special deed of gift,
After his death of all he dies possessed of.

LORENZO
295   Fair ladies, you drop manna in the way
Of starvèd people.

PORTIA
                          It is almost morning,
And yet I am sure you are not satisfied
Of these events at full. Let us go in,
And charge us there upon interr'gatories,
300   And we will answer all things faithfully.

GRATIANO
Let it be so. The first interr'gatory
That my Nerissa shall be sworn on is
Whether till the next night she had rather stay,
Or go to bed now, being two hours to day.
305   But were the day come, I should wish it dark,
That I were couching with the doctor's clerk.
Well, while I live I'll fear no other thing
So sore as keeping safe Nerissa's ring.

Exeunt

PORTIA

How are you, Lorenzo? My clerk has some comforting news for you, too.

NERISSA

Yes, and I'll give it to him for free. *(she gives* LORENZO *a document)* This is from the rich Jew, for you and Jessica. It's a special testament. After he dies, you'll inherit everything he owns.

LORENZO

Ladies, you're dropping bread from the heavens to starving people.

PORTIA

It's almost morning, but I'm sure you're not fully satisfied about what happened. Let's go inside and we'll answer all your questions truthfully.

GRATIANO

All right, then. My first question for Nerissa is whether she'd rather wait till tomorrow night or go to bed now, since there are only two more hours till morning. When the day comes, I'll wish it were nighttime, so I could sleep with the legal expert's clerk. In any case, I won't worry about anything for the rest of my life more than keeping Nerissa's ring safe.

They exit.

NOTES

PART III

STUDY
GUIDE

6

THEMATIC QUESTIONS

1. Discuss Shylock's dramatic function in *The Merchant of Venice*. What do critics mean when they suggest that Shylock is "too large" for the play? Does he fulfill or exceed his role?

In order to ensure that we understand Shylock as a threat to the happiness of Venice's citizens and lovers, Shakespeare uses a number of dramatic devices to amplify Shylock's villainy. In doing so, however, he creates a character so compelling that many feel Shylock comes to dominate the play, thereby making him "too large." Certainly, Shylock is a masterful creation. At his cruelest, he is terrifying, even more so because all of his schemes exist within the framework of the law. Seen in this light, Shylock becomes a kind of bogeyman, turning Venetian society's own institutions on themselves. On the other hand, Shylock is also pitiable, even sympathetic, at times. He has been harshly handled by Venetian society and has seen his daughter elope with one of the same men who despise him. His passionate monologue in Act Three, Scene 1 reveals that he feels the same emotions as his opponents, and we cannot help but see him as a man. In fact, Shylock's character is so well-rounded and intricate that many see him as the only interesting figure in a play that is not, in theory, supposed to center about him. Shylock's scenes are gripping and fascinating, and many critics believe the play deflates every time he makes an exit.

2. In the end, how comic is *The Merchant of Venice*? Does the final act succeed in restoring comedy to the play?

The Merchant of Venice contains all of the elements required of a Shakespearean comedy, but is often so overshadowed by the character of Shylock and his quest for a pound of flesh that it is hard not to find in the play a generous share of the tragic as well. Lovers pine and are reunited, a foolish servant makes endless series of puns, and genteel women masquerade as men—all of which are defining marks of Shakespearean comedy. In sharp contrast to these elements, however, Shakespeare also presents Shylock, a degraded old man who has lost his daughter and is consumed with a bloody greed. The light language of the play's comedic moments disappears for whole scenes at a time, and Antonio's fate is more suspenseful than funny. The final act redeems the play's claims to be a comedy, piling on the necessary humor and serendipity, but the rest of the play is overcast by the fact that Antonio may soon pay Bassanio's debt with his life.

3. Discuss the relationship between Jessica and Shylock. Are we meant to sympathize with the moneylender's daughter? Does Shakespeare seem ambivalent in his portrayal of Jessica?

In looking at the relationship between Jessica and Shylock, we are again forced to walk a fine line between sympathizing with and despising Shylock. For all intents and purposes, the play should label Shylock's mistreatment by his own daughter as richly deserved. After all, he is spiteful, petty, and mean; and in his more cartoonish or evil moments, it is hard to imagine why Jessica should stay. At other times, however, Jessica's escape seems like another cruel circumstance inflicted on Shylock, and her behavior offstage borders on heartless. Shylock is never more sympathetic than when he bemoans the fact that Jessica has taken a ring given to him in his bachelor days by his wife and has traded it for a monkey, the most banal of objects. Nor is Jessica ever able to produce satisfactory evidence that life in her father's house is miserable. Her seeming indifference to Antonio's fate—she and Lorenzo are more interested in the price of bacon—makes us wonder whether Jessica is actually more selfish and self-absorbed than the father she condemns. While Shylock is no saint, his resolve to collect his debt only seems to strengthen beyond reason after he discovers that Jessica has fled.

7

KEY QUESTIONS
AND ANSWERS

1. Why does Shylock demand Antonio's flesh instead of money?

Shylock is offered large sums of money in exchange for forfeiting the original conditions of his bond. He refuses to accept this offer, and he also refuses to justify his decision. As Shylock explains, "You'll ask me why I rather choose to have / A weight of carrion flesh than to receive / Three thousand ducats. I'll not answer that/But say it is my humour" (4.1.). Shylock argues that because he has the force of law on his side, he does not have to explain or justify his decision, and frames it as a kind of whim or impulse. It seems likely, however, that some of his extreme insistence on Antonio's flesh comes from his desire to have revenge against a member of the Christian community that he blames for discriminating against him, and stealing his daughter. When Salarino points out that flesh will be useless, Shylock counters by replying that "If it will feed nothing else, it will feed my revenge" (3.1.).

2. Why does Antonio agree to Shylock's terms for the loan?

When Shylock first states the terms he proposes for the loan, Antonio immediately accepts without any questions or doubts. Bassanio is the one to hesitate, urging his friend not to accept these dangerous terms: "You shall not seal to such a bond for me! / I'll rather dwell in my necessity" (1.3.). Antonio is confident that the terms of the loan are irrelevant because he will easily be able to pay it back. As he explains, "I do expect return / Of thrice three times the value of this bond" (1.3.). Because Antonio has always been prosperous and enjoyed good returns on his investment, he is lured into a false sense of security and does not worry about the risks he is assuming. His intense devotion to Bassanio also makes him willing to accept almost any risk in order to help his friend.

3. Who does Bassanio give Portia's ring to?

Bassanio gives Portia's ring to someone he believes is a lawyer named Balthazar, but who the audience knows is actually Portia herself in disguise as a man. Balthazar/Portia asks for the ring as a thank-you gift in exchange for having saved Antonio, and Bassanio is initially reluctant, because he promised never to take the ring off. As Bassanio explains, "There's more depends on this than on the value. / The dearest ring in Venice will I give you" (4.1.). However, after Balthazar/Portia rebukes him and Antonio encourages him to give the ring away, Bassanio relents.

4. How does Bassanio win the right to marry Portia?

Bassanio wins the right to marry Portia because he solves the riddle and correctly chooses the right casket. While the other suitors have incorrectly chosen the gold or silver casket, Bassanio chooses the lead casket and finds a picture of Portia inside, signaling that he can claim her as his bride. Bassanio's choice indicates that he is clever and not easily distracted by superficial charms. As the scroll inside the lead casket explains, "You that choose not by the view, / Chance as fair and choose as true."(3.2.). Portia, who has already fallen in love with Bassanio, is delighted when he chooses correctly, exclaiming "O love, be moderate. Allay thy ecstasy" (3.2.).

5. Why can't Antonio pay back his loan?

After a series of accidents, all of Antonio's ships are reported as wrecked. As Bassanio laments, "Have all his ventures failed? What, not one hit? ... not one vessel, scape the dreadful touch / Of merchant-marring rocks?" (3.2.). Antonio therefore does not have the money to pay Shylock back, and is in danger of having to pay the penalty of a pound of his own flesh. The swift change of fortune indicates the role of fate and luck in the play: Antonio was initially confident that his investment was guaranteed, but learns the hard way that nothing is ever certain. Thanks to Portia's generosity, Antonio gains enough money to be able to pay back the loan and even provide additional payment, but by then Shylock is insistent on claiming the penalty that he is technically owed. Later in the play we learn that in fact not all the ships went down, and Antonio is a rich man again.

8

THEMES, MOTIFS,
AND SYMBOLS

Themes

Themes are the fundamental and often universal ideas explored in a literary work.

SELF-INTEREST VERSUS LOVE

On the surface, the main difference between the Christian characters and Shylock appears to be that the Christian characters value human relationships over business ones, whereas Shylock is only interested in money. The Christian characters certainly view the matter this way. Merchants like Antonio lend money free of interest and put themselves at risk for those they love, whereas Shylock agonizes over the loss of his money and is reported to run through the streets crying, "O my ducats! O my daughter!" (2.8.). With these words, he apparently values his money at least as much as his daughter, suggesting that his greed outweighs his love. However, upon closer inspection, this supposed difference between Christian and Jew breaks down. When we see Shylock in Act Three, scene 1, he seems more hurt by the fact that his daughter sold a ring that was given to him by his dead wife before they were married than he is by the loss of the ring's monetary value. Some human relationships do indeed matter to Shylock more than money. Moreover, his insistence that he have a pound of flesh rather than any amount of money shows that his resentment is much stronger than his greed.

Just as Shylock's character seems hard to pin down, the Christian characters also present an inconsistent picture. Though Portia and Bassanio come to love one another, Bassanio seeks her hand in the first place because he is monstrously in debt and needs her money. Bassanio even asks Antonio to look at the money he lends Bassanio as an investment, though Antonio insists that he lends him the money solely out of love. In other words, Bassanio is anxious to view his relationship with Antonio as a matter of business rather than of love. Finally, Shylock eloquently argues that Jews are human beings just as Christians are, but Christians such as Antonio hate Jews simply because they are Jews. Thus, while the Christian characters may talk more about mercy, love, and charity, they are not always consistent in how they display these qualities.

THE DIVINE QUALITY OF MERCY

The conflict between Shylock and the Christian characters comes to a head over the issue of mercy. The other characters acknowledge that the law is on Shylock's side, but they all expect him to show mercy, which he refuses to do. When, during the trial, Shylock asks Portia what could possibly compel him to be merciful, Portia's long reply, beginning with the words, "The quality of mercy is not strained," clarifies what is at stake in the argument (4.1.). Human beings should be merciful because God is merciful: mercy is an attribute of God himself and therefore greater than power, majesty, or law. Portia's understanding of mercy is based on the way Christians in Shakespeare's time understood the difference between the Old and New Testaments. According to the writings of St. Paul in the New Testament, the Old Testament depicts God as requiring strict adherence to rules and exacting harsh punishments for those who stray. The New Testament, in contrast, emphasizes adherence to the spirit rather than the letter of the law, portraying a God who forgives rather than punishes and offers salvation to those followers who forgive others. Thus, when Portia warns Shylock against pursuing the law without regard for mercy, she is promoting what Elizabethan Christians would have seen as a pro-Christian, anti-Jewish agenda.

The strictures of Renaissance drama demanded that Shylock be a villain, and, as such, patently unable to show even a drop of compassion for his enemy. A sixteenth-century audience would not expect Shylock to exercise mercy—therefore, it is up to the Christians to do so. Once she has turned Shylock's greatest weapon—the law—against him, Portia has the opportunity to give freely of the mercy for which she so beautifully advocates. Instead, she backs Shylock into a corner, where she strips him of his bond, his estate, and his dignity, forcing him to kneel and beg for mercy. Given that Antonio decides not to seize Shylock's goods as punishment for conspiring against him, we might consider Antonio to be merciful. But we may also question whether it is merciful to return to Shylock half of his goods, only to take away his religion and his profession. By forcing Shylock to convert, Antonio disables him from practicing usury, which, according to Shylock's reports, was Antonio's primary reason for berating and spitting on him in public. Antonio's compassion, then, seems to stem as much from self-interest as from concern for his fellow man. Mercy, as delivered in *The Merchant of Venice*, never manages to be as sweet, selfless, or full of grace as Portia presents it.

HATRED AS A CYCLICAL PHENOMENON

Throughout the play, Shylock claims that he is simply applying the lessons taught to him by his Christian neighbors; this claim becomes an integral part of both his character and his argument in court. In Shylock's very first appearance, as he conspires to harm Antonio, his entire plan seems to be born of the insults and injuries Antonio has inflicted upon him in the past. As the play continues, and Shylock unveils more of his reasoning, the same idea rears its head over and over—he is simply applying what years of abuse have taught him. Responding to Salarino's query of what good the pound of flesh will do him, Shylock responds, "The villainy you teach me I will execute—and it shall go hard but I will better the instruction" (3.1.). Not all of Shylock's actions can be blamed on poor teachings, and one could argue that Antonio understands his own culpability in his near-execution. With the trial's conclusion, Antonio demands that Shylock convert to Christianity, but inflicts no other punishment, despite the threats of fellow Christians like Gratiano. Antonio does not, as he has in the past, kick or spit on Shylock. Antonio, as well as the duke, effectively ends the conflict by starving it of the injustices it needs to continue.

Motifs

Motifs are recurring structures, contrasts, and literary devices that can help to develop and inform the text's major themes.

THE LAW

The Merchant of Venice depends heavily upon laws and rules— the laws of the state of Venice and the rules stipulated in contracts and wills. Laws and rules can be manipulated for cruel or wanton purposes, but they are also capable of producing good when executed by the right people. Portia's virtual imprisonment by the game of caskets seems, at first, like a questionable rule at best, but her likening of the game to a lottery system is belied by the fact that, in the end, it works perfectly. The game keeps a host of suitors at bay, and of the three who try to choose the correct casket to win Portia's hand, only the man of Portia's desires succeeds. By the time Bassanio picks the correct chest, the choice seems like a more efficient indicator of human nature than any person could ever provide. A similar phenomenon occurs with Venetian law. Until Portia's arrival, Shylock is the law's strictest adherent, and it seems as if the city's adherence to contracts will result in tragedy. However, when Portia arrives and manipulates the law most skillfully of all, the outcome is the happiest ending of all, at least to an Elizabethan audience: Antonio is rescued and Shylock forced to abandon his religion. The fact that the trial is such a close call does, however, raise the fearful specter of how the law can be misused. Without the proper guidance, the law can be wielded to do horrible things.

CROSS-DRESSING

Twice in the play, daring escapes are executed with the help of crossdressing. Jessica escapes the tedium of Shylock's house by dressing as a page, while Portia and Nerissa rescue Antonio by posing as officers of the Venetian court. This device was not only familiar to Renaissance drama, but essential to its performance:

women were banned from the stage and their parts were performed by prepubescent boys. Shakespeare was a great fan of the potentials of cross-dressing and used the device often, especially in his comedies. But Portia reveals that the donning of men's clothes is more than mere comedy. She says that she has studied a "thousand raw tricks of these bragging jacks," implying that male authority is a kind of performance that can be imitated successfully (3.1.). She feels confident that she can outwit any male competitor, declaring, "I'll prove the prettier fellow of the two, / And wear my dagger with the braver grace" (3.4.). In short, by assuming the clothes of the opposite sex, Portia enables herself to assume the power and position denied to her as a woman.

FILIAL PIETY

Like Shakespeare's other comedies, *The Merchant of Venice* seems to endorse the behavior of characters who treat filial piety lightly, even though the heroine, Portia, sets the opposite example by obeying her father's will. Launcelot greets his blind, long-lost father by giving the old man confusing directions and telling the old man that his beloved son Launcelot is dead. This moment of impertinence can be excused as essential to the comedy of the play, but it sets the stage for Jessica's far more complex hatred of her father. Jessica can list no specific complaints when she explains her desire to leave Shylock's house, and in the one scene in which she appears with Shylock, he fusses over her in a way that some might see as tender. Jessica's desire to leave is made clearer when the other characters note how separate she has become from her father, but her behavior after departing seems questionable at best. Most notably, she trades her father's ring, given to him by her dead mother, for a monkey. The frivolity of this exchange, in which an heirloom is tossed away for the silliest of objects, makes for quite a disturbing image of the esteem in which *The Merchant of Venice's* children hold their parents, and puts us, at least temporarily, in Shylock's corner.

Symbols

Symbols are objects, characters, figures, and colors used to represent abstract ideas or concepts.

THE THREE CASKETS

The contest for Portia's hand, in which suitors from various countries choose among a gold, a silver, and a lead casket, resembles the cultural and legal system of Venice in some respects. Like the Venice of the play, the casket contest presents the same opportunities and the same rules to men of various nations, ethnicities, and religions. Also like Venice, the hidden bias of the casket test is fundamentally Christian. To win Portia, Bassanio must ignore the gold casket, which bears the inscription, "Who chooseth me shall gain what many men desire" (2.8.), and the silver casket, which says, "Who chooseth me shall get as much as he deserves" (2.8.). The correct casket is lead and warns that the person who chooses it must give and risk everything he has. The contest combines a number of Christian teachings, such as the idea that desire is an unreliable guide and should be resisted, and the idea that human beings do not deserve God's grace but receive it in spite of themselves. Christianity teaches that appearances are often deceiving, and that people should not trust the evidence provided by the senses—hence the humble appearance of the lead casket. Faith and charity are the central values of Christianity, and these values are evoked by the lead casket's injunction to give all and risk all, as one does in making a leap of faith. Portia's father has presented marriage as one in which the proper suitor risks and gives everything for the spouse, in the hope of a divine recompense he can never truly deserve. The contest certainly suits Bassanio, who knows he does not deserve his good fortune but is willing to risk everything on a gamble.

THE POUND OF FLESH

The pound of flesh that Shylock seeks lends itself to multiple interpretations: it emerges most as a metaphor for two of the play's closest relationships, but also calls attention to Shylock's inflexible adherence to the law. The fact that Bassanio's debt is to be paid with Antonio's flesh is significant, showing how their friendship is so binding it has made them almost one. Shylock's determination is strengthened by Jessica's departure, as if he were seeking recompense for the loss of his own flesh and blood by collecting it from his enemy. Lastly, the pound of flesh is a constant reminder of the rigidity of Shylock's world, where numerical calculations are used to evaluate even the most serious of situations. Shylock never explicitly demands that Antonio die, but asks instead, in his numerical mind, for a pound in exchange for his three thousand ducats. Where the other characters measure their emotions with long metaphors and words, Shylock measures everything in far more prosaic and numerical quantities.

LEAH'S RING

The ring given to Shylock in his bachelor days by a woman named Leah, who is most likely Shylock's wife and Jessica's mother, gets only a brief mention in the play, but is still an object of great importance. When told that Jessica has stolen it and traded it for a monkey, Shylock very poignantly laments its loss: "I would not have given it for a wilderness of monkeys" (3.1.). The lost ring allows us to see Shylock in an uncharacteristically vulnerable position and to view him as a human being capable of feeling something more than anger. Although Shylock and Tubal discuss the ring for no more than five lines, the ring stands as an important symbol of Shylock's humanity, his ability to love, and his ability to grieve.

9

QUOTES AND ANALYSIS BY THEME

FRIENDSHIP

My purse, my person, my extremest means

Lie all unlocked to your occasions. (1.1.)

After Bassanio approaches Antonio with his plan to get out of debt, Antonio tells him that he would sacrifice anything to help before even hearing the details of Bassanio's plan. In this moment, we're introduced to Antonio's unwavering dedication to Bassanio, which motivates Antonio to take a risky loan from Shylock for Bassanio's benefit two scenes later. Antonio's decision to borrow money from Shylock, which stems from the strength of his love for his friend, drives the plot of the entire play.

Well, jailer, on.—Pray God Bassanio come

To see me pay his debt, and then I care not. (3.3.)

Captured by Shylock and the jailer for defaulting on his loan, Antonio resigns himself to death, expressing the desire to see Bassanio before he dies. Because this combination of love and tragedy feels characteristic of romantic love, not love between friends, moments like this have made some scholars speculate that Antonio's sadness might come from unrequited romantic feelings toward Bassanio. Either way, the intensity of Antonio's feelings for Bassanio drives his decisions throughout the play.

The Jew shall have my flesh, blood, bones and all,

Ere thou shalt lose for me one drop of blood. (4.1.)

Right before Portia enters the trial scene to save Antonio, Bassanio encourages Antonio to be brave, declaring that he will defend him from Shylock with everything he has. This declaration of friendship mirrors the one Antonio made for Bassanio in the first scene of the play ("my purse, my person, my extremest means . . ."), in both structure and intensity, showing us that friendship is a value that shapes Bassanio's decisions, actions, and worldview just as it shapes the way Antonio lives.

> *Antonio, I am married to a wife*
>
> *Which is as dear to me as life itself.*
>
> *But life itself, my wife, and all the world*
>
> *Are not with me esteemed above thy life. (4.1.)*

Bassanio makes his ultimate proclamation of love to Antonio at the climax of the trial scene, when it seems as though Portia, disguised at Balthazar, will allow Shylock to cut the pound of flesh from Antonio's chest. His claim that his love for his friend is greater than his love for both his wife and for life itself stresses the importance of friendship in the world of the play. The bond between friends governs the way these men think, speak, and act, shaping the course of the play.

WEALTH

> *And every object that might make me fear*
>
> *Misfortune to my ventures out of doubt*
>
> *Would make me sad. (1.1.)*

In the first scene of the play, Solanio speculates that Antonio might be sad because his wealth is tied up in ships, which can be risky investments. That money problems are his first thought, not family problems, romantic problems, or any other kind of personal crisis, suggests that money and wealth dominate the lives and minds of these Venetians. Though Antonio goes on to deny that his sadness stems from anxiety about his investments, the way that problems of wealth influence the course of the play confirms the importance of money and wealth in this Venetian society.

> *I never heard a passion so confused,*
>
> *So strange, outrageous, and so variable*
>
> *As the dog Jew did utter in the streets.*
>
> *"My daughter! O my ducats! O my daughter! (2.8.)*

Solanio recounts Shylock's reaction of Jessica's disappearance to Salarino with disgust, describing Shylock as subhuman because of his supposed preoccupation with money over family. This moment exemplifies the hypocrisy of the Christian community's hatred for Shylock; they condemn him for seeking wealth, yet they are equally preoccupied with their finances. Solanio recognizes the worst of himself and his community in Shylock's greed, so he and his friends make Shylock into a villain to distance themselves.

> *For herein Fortune shows herself more kind*
>
> *Than is her custom. It is still her use*
>
> *To let the wretched man outlive his wealth. (4.1.)*

Antonio tells his friends not to grieve his death after Portia, disguised as Balthazar, asks him for a few last words before Shylock harvests his pound of flesh. He explains that he's better off dead anyway since all his business ventures have failed, implying that he considers wealth to be the most important part of life despite his speeches about friendship and his condemnation of Shylock's greed. The paradox of revelation is that Antonio finds himself in this position because he valued his friendship with Bassanio over his finances.

> *You take my house when you do take the prop*
>
> *That doth sustain my house. You take my life*
>
> *When you do take the means whereby I live. (4.1.)*

During Shylock's sentencing, he makes a pragmatic argument for wealth, explaining that, in a commercial society like Venice, a person cannot pursue nobler values such a family, friendship, or love without being financially secure. If a person values their life, they must value money, the means by which they live. Unlike the Christian men of Venetian society, trying to appear above valuing wealth doesn't preoccupy him. Shylock sees wealth as intractable in the pursuit of life, while the Christian merchants follow a code of manners that forces them to pretend that worrying about money is beneath them.

> *He is well paid that is well satisfied. (4.1.)*

Portia, disguised as Balthazar, refuses payment from Bassanio and Antonio after she defeats Shylock in court. She reasons that the satisfaction of doing right is payment enough for her. Portia, who lives in Belmont, does not live by the same values as the men of Venetian commerce. In Venice, money is paramount, while in Belmont human interaction, such as love, rules.

PREJUDICE

> *If he have the condition a saint and the complexion of*
> *a devil, I had rather he should shrive me than wive*
> *me. (1.2.)*

In just scene two of act one, Portia tells Nerissa that even if the Prince of Morocco behaves perfectly, she still wouldn't be interested in marrying him, because of his dark complexion. This sets a precedent continued through the rest of the play: the play's protagonists act on prejudice against those who look or act differently than they do. As Portia's prejudice is an inextricable factor in her search for a husband, the plot-shaping actions of characters such as Antonio, Bassanio, Lorenzo, and Launcelot are laced with a prejudice that troubles modern readers.

> *You call me misbeliever, cutthroat dog,*
> *And spet upon my Jewish gaberdine. (1.3.)*

When Antonio and Bassanio approach Shylock for a loan, Shylock recounts Antonio's past abuse. These vivid images of Antonio's anti-Semitic cruelty explain the origin of Shylock's hatred for Antonio and his friends. Because of this, no matter how villainous Shylock becomes, modern readers can't simply root for the play's protagonists, because we've witnessed their cruelty. Some interpretations of the play argue that moments such as this are evidence that Shakespeare intended Shylock to be a victim, not a villain, while others claim that those arguments come from a modern understanding of prejudice and shouldn't be applied to an Elizabethan text.

> *This making of Christians will raise the price of hogs.*
> *(3.5.)*

Launcelot teases Jessica about her conversion from Judaism to Christianity. Despite running away from Shylock, marrying Lorenzo, and converting to Christianity, Jessica remains subject to anti-Semitism because the attitude is so deeply ingrained in the play's Christian characters. For modern readers analyzing and interpreting this play, this moment demonstrates the strength of prejudice in the thoughts and actions of the characters, reminding us take the historical context of the play into account when making inferences about characterization and motivation.

REVENGE

> *If I can catch him once upon the hip,*
> *I will feed fat the ancient grudge I bear him. (1.3.)*

In an aside during the third scene of the play when Bassanio and Antonio approach Shylock for the loan, Shylock describes the reasons he hates Antonio, ending with this description of revenge. His use of "ancient" references a history of anti-Semitism in Europe much older than him and Antonio, and "feed fat" is an example of the base, animal language that characterizes Shylock as gruesome and monstrous. This aside sets up Shylock's main motivation for the play, which is revenge on Antonio as a symbol for revenge on a society that has wronged him and his ancestors.

> *The villainy you teach me I will execute, and it shall*
>
> *go hard but I will better the instruction. (3.1.)*

In the final line of Shylock's famous "hath not a Jew eyes?" speech, Shylock describes the nature of revenge as a never-ending and intensifying cycle. He demonstrates that he understands that killing Antonio would be a larger crime than Antonio's offenses against him, but prefers it that way. In this line Shylock simultaneously validates his desire for revenge, explaining that he's only a villain because Antonio and his friends have taught him to be that way through their cruelty, and condemns it, explaining how he would take pleasure in a greater punishment for Antonio.

> *Thou shalt have justice more than thou desirest. (4.1.)*

Just before Portia, disguised as Balthazar during the trial scene, delivers her verdict, she tells Shylock that he will have more justice than he wants. The phrase "more justice" stands in for punishment. This line sets us Portia's verdict as Shylock's punishment for trying to collect the terms of his loan, or revenge for trying to kill Antonio. Portia, like Shylock, acts out of a desire for revenge against those who threaten her tribe, showing that the attitude permeates the play.

10

QUOTES AND ANALYSIS
BY CHARACTER

SHYLOCK

> *I will buy with you, sell with you, talk with you, walk*
> *with you, and so following, but I will not eat with you,*
> *drink with you, nor pray with you. (1.3.)*

Shylock speaks these lines in an aside after Bassanio, who is trying to secure a loan, invites him to dinner. Shylock makes it clear that he does not actually like or trust the Christians, and does not feel that he has much in common with them. He relies on business relationships in order to prosper in his profession, but has no desire to form genuine friendships with any of the Venetian Christians.

> *I hate him for he is a Christian. (1.3.)*

Shylock speaks these lines in reference to Antonio. This quote shows Shylock's deep-seated prejudice and bitterness, and hints that Shylock is looking for ways to harm characters like Antonio and Bassanio even as he engages in business dealings with them.

> *Another time*
> *You called me "dog"; and for these courtesies*
> *I'll lend you thus much moneys? (1.3.)*

Shylock complains about how he has previously been mistreated and abused, but is now being sought out to provide services for the Christian merchant. These lines are important because they illustrate the double standard faced by Shylock and many other Jewish professionals at the time. Shylock is criticized for lending money and charging interest, a practice that contradicted Christian doctrine; but at the same time, moneylending was essential to Venetian business practices.

> Nor thrust your head into the public street
>
> To gaze on Christian fools with varnished faces. (2.5.)

Shylock warns his daughter Jessica to stay inside while he is absent from the house. The lines show that Shylock is suspicious of the Christian population, and that he may have a sense of foreshadowing that his daughter is plotting something. The lines create dramatic irony, because the audience knows, but Shylock does not, that Jessica plans to elope with a Christian that very night.

> If it will feed nothing else, it will feed my revenge. (3.1.)

Shylock speaks this line after Solarino suggests there is no point to Shylock claiming his bond. Although he agrees that the flesh has no financial or business value, Shylock says he will feel a vengeful pleasure in hurting a man associated with the Christian community. The quote shows Shylock's deep and malicious hatred of Antonio and the other Christians.

> If you prick us, do we not bleed? If you tickle us, do
>
> we not laugh? If you poison us, do we not die? (3.1.)

Shylock explains why he is justified in hating Christians and seeking revenge. He argues that he and many other Jews have been consistently degraded and abused, and that it is only reasonable that he would now want to seize the opportunity to lash out. These lines suggest that Shylock believes Jews and Christians are not actually so different from one another.

> You take my life
>
> When you do take the means whereby I live. (4.1.)

Shylock speaks these lines to the court when he learns he is going to have to forfeit his estate as part of the penalty imposed on him. The quote conveys his intense obsession with earning money and accumulating wealth. At the same time, the quote can be read sympathetically, because Shylock is justifiably lamenting that he is about to lose everything.

PORTIA

> *I can easier teach twenty what were good to be done*
>
> *than to be one of the twenty to follow mine own*
>
> *teaching. (1.2.)*

Portia laments her frustration with the conditions her father imposed on her marriage. Portia would like to be able to freely choose who to marry, but she also feels obligated to honor her father's wishes. The tension between what she believes to be right and what she actually wants to do drives her to complain that she would rather tell other people how to behave than behave that way herself.

> *If I live to be as old as Sibylla, I will die as chaste*
>
> *as Diana unless I be obtained by the manner of my*
>
> *father's will. (1.2.)*

Portia speaks these lines to Nerissa to articulate her commitment to keeping her promise. Even though she finds it challenging to have no say over who she marries, Portia is determined to act honorably. In the end, Portia's commitment to keeping her word is rewarded because the man she loves ends up being the successful suitor anyway.

> *I could teach you*
>
> *How to choose right, but I am then forsworn. (3.2.)*

Portia says these lines to Bassanio shortly before he attempts to solve the riddle. Because she wants Bassanio to choose correctly, Portia is tempted to help him, or give hints about how to guess. However, her sense of honor and integrity ultimately triumph, and she does not give Bassanio any clues.

STUDY GUIDE

> *But now I was the lord*
>
> *Of this fair mansion, master of my servants,*
>
> *Queen o'er myself. (3.2.)*

Portia says these lines to Bassanio after he solves the riddle, earning the right to marry her. She acknowledges that she was in a powerful position as a wealthy unmarried woman who could make decisions and exert authority. Now that she is getting married, she happily gives up this independence in order to be with Bassanio. This quote shows that although Portia values independence, she puts more value on love and companionship.

> *For never shall you lie by Portia's side*
>
> *With an unquiet soul. (3.2.)*

Portia reassures Bassanio that she is happy to give him money so that he can pay back his debt and save Antonio. Portia shows her generosity and desire to make sure her new husband always has everything he needs. The quote is important because it shows how the typical gender dynamic is reversed in this couple, where Portia is the one bestowing money on her husband and reassuring him that he will never have financial worries in the future.

> *The quality of mercy is not strained.*
>
> *It droppeth as the gentle rain from heaven. (4.1.)*

Portia speaks these lines in her famous courtroom speech as she urges Shylock to consider showing mercy to Antonio. The speech draws on traditional Christian teachings about the value of mercy and forgiveness, but it makes no impact on Shylock. The speech shows Portia as a highly intelligent and articulate character, but she is also only allowed to present her views in this public way because she is disguised as a man.

> *He is well paid that is well satisfied.*
>
> *And I, delivering you, am satisfied,*
>
> *And therein do account myself well paid. (4.1.)*

Portia speaks these lines while disguised as Balthazar, turning down the offer to take payment in exchange for her legal services. The audience knows she does not need payment because she is a wealthy heiress, but the lines also contrast Portia's behavior with Shylock's earlier actions. Portia suggests that money is not important to her, and that doing a good deed is reward enough, whereas Shylock has always insisted on getting exactly what he is owed.

> I'll not deny him anything I have,
>
> No, not my body, nor my husband's bed. (5.1.)

Portia playfully tricks Bassanio into believing that she intends to be unfaithful to him. Portia is pretending to be angry that Bassanio gave her ring to the lawyer, and her lines create a comedic effect because the audience knows that she herself is the lawyer she is talking about. The lines make her point that Bassanio should not have broken his promise and given up the ring.

ANTONIO

> In sooth, I know not why I am so sad. (1.1.)

At the beginning of the play Antonio explains that he feels sadness without knowing why. The quote positions him as a melancholy character and sets up his later willingness to passively accept his fate. It might seem strange that Antonio is so willing to accept his impending death, but if he has been sad and aimless the entire time, it makes sense he is not much attached to whether he lives or dies.

> A stage where every man must play a part,
>
> And mine a sad one. (1.1.)

Antonio speaks these lines to a group of friends, shrugging off the fact that it seems he is destined to always be unhappy. Antonio's acceptance of his sadness suggests he does not think there is anything he can do to improve his fate, and might be considered evidence for the possibility that he feels unrequited love for Bassanio.

My purse, my person, my extremest means

Lie all unlocked to your occasions. (1.1.)

Antonio vows to Bassanio that he will do anything to help his friend get the money he needs. The lines show that Antonio is a devoted friend, and possibly hint that his feelings for Bassanio may go beyond friendship. The quote also sets up the loyalty Antonio will show throughout the play, being willing to give anything to help Bassanio.

You may as well do anything most hard,

As seek to soften that—than which what's harder?—

His Jewish heart. (4.1.)

Antonio explains that there is no point trying to persuade Shylock to change his mind. The lines express the prejudice Antonio feels toward Shylock as a Jew, and how he connects Shylock's bloodthirsty desire for vengeance to his Jewish identity. The lines also show how Antonio is willing to passively accept his fate, and not even try to fight it.

BASSANIO

Gratiano speaks an infinite deal of nothing, more than

any man in all Venice. (1.1.)

Bassanio fondly jokes about his friend's noisy and high-spirited personality. The quote shows that Bassanio can accurately observe the nature of others and see both their strengths and weaknesses. This capacity for thoughtful observation will serve Bassanio well when he has to solve the riddle of the caskets.

My chief care

Is to come fairly off from the great debts. (1.1.)

Bassanio explains how he is trying to resolve his financial situation and fix the mistakes he has made. The quote shows that Bassanio is starting to grow up and think more about the future, rather than focusing solely on enjoying the present. However, in order for Bassanio to get out of debt, he first has to borrow even more money.

> Sometimes from her eyes
>
> I did receive fair speechless messages. (1.1.)

Bassanio hopes that Portia is attracted to him. At this point, he doesn't seem to know that he will have to solve a riddle in order to win her as his bride. The quote shows that Bassanio is somewhat strategic in his planning for how to solve his financial problems, but also that he is relying on uncertain factors.

> The world is still deceived with ornament. (3.2.)

Bassanio says this line as he contemplates which casket to choose. He knows that many people would assume the gold or silver to be the most valuable, but he is wise enough to know that shiny exteriors do not always accurately indicate the value inside. Bassanio's wisdom and shrewd nature lead him to make the right choice, and win the right to marry the woman he loves.

> When I told you
>
> My state was nothing, I should then have told you
>
> That I was worse than nothing. (3.2.)

Bassanio explains to Portia that he is indebted to Antonio. He feels a sense of shame at having to admit this truth to a wealthy and independent woman, and he also acknowledges the stigma around individuals who are in debt. The quote also shows, however, that he trusts Portia and feels comfortable being vulnerable with her.

GRATIANO

> With mirth and laughter let old wrinkles come. (1.1.)

Gratiano contrasts his own life philosophy with Antonio's melancholy disposition. Gratiano is focused on enjoying life as much as possible, and is not afraid of growing older as long as he brings his sense of fun with him. The quote shows that Gratiano is self-aware about what kind of life he wants and consciously cultivates a happy life for himself.

> *My eyes, my lord, can look as swift as yours.*
>
> *You saw the mistress, I beheld the maid. (3.2.)*

Gratiano says that he and Nerissa have fallen in love and want to get married. The quote shows that despite his light-hearted ways, he is capable of feeling deep love and choosing commitment. The line also shows how friendship can influence the choice of romantic partners: with the double marriage, all four friends can plan to enjoy a life together.

> *Can no prayers pierce thee? (4.1.)*

Gratiano implores Shylock to relent and show compassion to Antonio. The quote shows the anger and frustration Gratiano feels, and his passionate, out-spoken nature. The quote also offers an element of irony, since a Jewish character like Shylock would be unlikely to be moved by Christian prayers, yet Gratiano tries this strategy anyway.

CHAPTER

11

WHAT DOES
THE ENDING MEAN?

THE PLAY ENDS WITH BASSANIO, ANTONIO, AND GRATIANO
returning to Belmont to reunite with Portia and Nerissa, who have
just arrived from Venice themselves. Portia and Nerissa pretend
to be angry with their husbands for having given away the rings
they swore to cherish, but eventually the women reveal that they
were the ones to save Antonio while disguised as men. The ending contrasts with the serious themes that dominate much of the
play, focusing instead on playful teasing between lovers and the
promise of a happy resolution. The switch in location from Venice
to Belmont signals a shift in tone from the tension of the courtroom scenes to idyllic life on a beautiful estate, where everyone
ends up with their appropriate partner. Nonetheless, the ending
does include some thematic connections to earlier portions of the
play. The anger and betrayal that Portia and Nerissa pretend to
feel when they accuse their husbands of breaking their promises
echoes the theme of bonds and contracts. When Portia and Nerissa
lead the men to believe they have been unfaithful, Gratiano threatens to "mar the young clerk's pen" (5.1.). The men's anger echoes
Shylock's anger after Jessica runs away, suggesting the Christian
and Jewish characters have much in common.

NOTES

12

HOW TO WRITE
LITERARY ANALYSIS

WHEN YOU READ FOR PLEASURE, your only goal is enjoyment. You might find yourself reading to get caught up in an exciting story, to learn about an interesting time or place, or just to pass the time. Maybe you're looking for inspiration, guidance, or a reflection of your own life. There are as many different, valid ways of reading a book as there are books in the world.

When you read a work of literature in an English class, however, you're being asked to read in a special way: you're being asked to perform *literary analysis*. To analyze something means to break it down into smaller parts and then examine how those parts work, both individually and together. Literary analysis involves examining all the parts of a novel, play, short story, or poem—elements such as character, setting, tone, and imagery—and thinking about how the author uses those elements to create certain effects.

A LITERARY ESSAY IS NOT A BOOK REVIEW

You're not being asked whether or not you liked a book or whether you'd recommend it to another reader. A literary essay also isn't like the kind of book report you wrote when you were younger, where your teacher wanted you to summarize the book's action. A high school- or college-level literary essay asks, "How does this piece of literature actually work?" "How does it do what it does?" and, "Why might the author have made the choices he or she did?"

The Seven Steps

No one is born knowing how to analyze literature; it's a skill you learn and a process you can master. As you gain more practice with this kind of thinking and writing, you'll be able to craft a method that works best for you. But until then, here are seven basic steps to writing a well-constructed literary essay:

1. Ask questions

2. Collect evidence

3. Construct a thesis

4. Develop and organize arguments

5. Write the introduction

6. Write the body paragraphs

7. Write the conclusion

1. ASK QUESTIONS

When you're assigned a literary essay in class, your teacher will often provide you with a list of writing prompts. Lucky you! Now all you have to do is choose one. Do yourself a favor and pick a topic that interests you. You'll have a much better (not to mention easier) time if you start off with something you enjoy thinking about. If you are asked to come up with a topic by yourself, though, you might start to feel a little panicked. Maybe you have too many ideas—or none at all. Don't worry. Take a deep breath and start by asking yourself these questions:

What struck you? Did a particular image, line, or scene linger in your mind for a long time? If it fascinated you, chances are you can draw on it to write a fascinating essay.

What confused you? Maybe you were surprised to see a character act in a certain way, or maybe you didn't understand why the book ended the way it did. Confusing moments in a work of literature are like a loose thread in a sweater: if you pull on it, you can unravel the entire thing. Ask yourself why the author chose to write about that character or scene the way he or she did and you might tap into some important insights about the work as a whole.

Did you notice any patterns? Is there a phrase that the main character uses constantly or an image that repeats throughout the book? If you can figure out how that pattern weaves through the work and what the significance of that pattern is, you've almost got your entire essay mapped out.

Did you notice any contradictions or ironies? Great works of literature are complex; great literary essays recognize and explain those complexities. Maybe the title totally disagrees with the book's subject matter. Maybe the main character acts one way around his family and a completely different way around his friends and associates. If you can find a way to explain a work's contradictory elements, you've got the seeds of a great essay.

At this point, you don't need to know exactly what you're going to say about your topic; you just need a place to begin your exploration. You can help direct your reading and brainstorming by formulating your topic as a *question*, which you'll then try to answer in your essay. The best questions invite critical debates and discussions, not just a rehashing of the summary. Remember, you're looking for something you can *prove* or *argue* based on evidence you find in the text. Finally, remember to keep the scope of your question in mind. Is this a topic you can adequately address within the word or page limit you've been given? Conversely, is this a topic big enough to fill the required length?

GOOD QUESTIONS

> *"Are Romeo and Juliet's parents responsible for the deaths of their children?"*

> *"Why doesn't Hamlet kill Claudius right away?"*

> *"Is Lady Macbeth a villain, or a victim?"*

BAD QUESTIONS

> *"What happens to Nick Bottom in* A Midsummer Night's Dream*?"*

> *"What do the other characters in* Julius Caesar *think about Caesar?"*

> *"How does Iago remind me of my brother?"*

2. COLLECT EVIDENCE

Once you know what question you want to answer, it's time to scour the book for things that will help you answer it. Don't worry if you don't know what you want to say yet—right now you're just collecting ideas and material and letting it all percolate. Keep track of passages, symbols, images, or scenes that deal with your topic. Eventually, you'll start making connections between these examples, and your thesis will emerge.

Here's a brief summary of the various parts that compose each and every work of literature. These are the elements that you will analyze in your essay, and that you will offer as evidence to support your arguments.

ELEMENTS OF STORY

These are the *whats* of the work—what happens, where it happens, and to whom it happens.

Plot: All of the events and actions of the work.

Character: The people who act and are acted upon in a literary work. The main character of a work is known as the *protagonist*.

Conflict: The central tension in the work. In most cases, the protagonist wants something, while opposing forces (antagonists) hinder the protagonist's progress.

Setting: When and where the work takes place. Elements of setting include location, time period, time of day, weather, social atmosphere, and economic conditions.

Narrator: The person telling the story. The narrator may straightforwardly report what happens, convey the subjective opinions and perceptions of one or more characters, or provide commentary and opinion in his or her own voice.

Themes: The main idea or message of the work—usually an abstract idea about people, society, or life in general. A work may have many themes, which may be in conflict with one another.

ELEMENTS OF STYLE

These are the *hows*—how the characters speak, how the story is constructed, and how language is used throughout the work.

Structure and organization: *How the parts of the work are assembled.* Some novels are narrated in a linear, chronological fashion, while others skip around in time. Some plays follow a traditional three- or five-act structure, while others are a series of loosely connected scenes. Some authors deliberately leave gaps in their works, leaving readers to puzzle out the missing information. A work's structure and organization can tell you a lot about the kind of message it wants to convey.

Point of view: *The perspective from which a story is told.* In *first-person point of view*, the narrator involves him- or herself in the story. ("I went to the store"; "We watched in horror as the bird slammed into the window.") A first-person narrator is usually the protagonist of the work, but not always. In *third-person point of view*, the narrator does not participate in the story. A third-person narrator may closely follow a specific character, recounting that individual character's thoughts or experiences, or it may be what we call an *omniscient* narrator. Omniscient narrators see and know all: they can witness any event in any time or place and are privy to the inner thoughts and feelings of all characters. Remember that the narrator and the author are not the same thing!

Diction: *Word choice.* Whether a character uses dry, clinical language or flowery prose with lots of exclamation points can tell you a lot about his or her attitude and personality.

Syntax: *Word order and sentence construction.* Syntax is a crucial part of establishing an author's narrative voice. Shakespeare, for example, is known for writing in iambic pentameter, intermingling prose and verse, and scrambling the usual word order of a sentence.

Tone: *The mood or feeling of the text.* Diction and syntax often contribute to the tone of a work. A novel written in short, clipped sentences that use small, simple words might feel brusque, cold, or matter-of-fact.

Imagery: *Language that appeals to the senses;* representing things that can be seen, smelled, heard, tasted, or touched.

Figurative language: *Language that is not meant to be interpreted literally.* The most common types of figurative language are *metaphors* and *similes*, which compare two unlike things in order to suggest a similarity between them —for example, *"All the world's a stage,"* or *"I'll warrant him, as gentle as a lamb."* (Metaphors say one thing *is* another thing; similes claim that one thing is *like* another thing.)

3. CONSTRUCT A THESIS

When you've examined all the evidence you've collected and know how you want to answer the question, it's time to write your thesis statement. A *thesis* is a claim about a work of literature that needs to be supported by evidence and arguments. The thesis statement is the heart of the literary essay, and the bulk of your essay will be spent trying to prove this claim. A good thesis will be:

> **Arguable.** *"Julius Caesar* describes the political turmoil in Rome after the murder of Julius Caesar" isn't a thesis—it's a fact.

> **Provable through textual evidence.** *"Hamlet* is a confusing but ultimately very well-written play" is a weak thesis because it offers the writer's personal opinion about the book. Yes, it's arguable, but it's not a claim that can be proved or supported with examples taken from the play itself.

> **Surprising.** "Viola changes a great deal in *Twelfth Night"* is a weak thesis because it's obvious. A really strong thesis will argue for a reading of the text that is not immediately apparent.

> **Specific.** "The relationships in *A Midsummer Night's Dream* tell us a lot about the fickle nature of romance" is almost a good thesis statement, but it's still too vague. What does the writer mean by "a lot"? How do the relationships tell us about the fickle nature of romance?

GOOD THESIS STATEMENTS

Question: In *Romeo and Juliet*, which is more powerful in shaping the lovers' story: fate or foolishness?

Thesis: "Though Shakespeare defines Romeo and Juliet as 'star-crossed lovers' and images of stars and planets appear throughout the play, a closer examination of that celestial imagery reveals that the stars are merely witnesses to the characters' foolish activities and not the causes themselves."

Question: Does Hamlet's misogyny prove his madness?

Thesis: "Hamlet's misogynistic behavior toward Gertrude and Ophelia can be seen as evidence that he really is going mad, because these scenes have little to do with his quest for justice, and yet they seem to provoke his strongest feelings. We see little evidence in the play that either Gertrude or Ophelia is guilty of any wrongdoing, yet he treats them both with paranoia and cruelty, suggesting that he has lost the ability to accurately interpret other people's motivations."

Question: How does blood function as a symbol in *Macbeth*?

Thesis: "Once Macbeth and Lady Macbeth embark on their murderous journey, blood comes to symbolize their guilt, and they begin to feel that their crimes have stained them in a way that cannot be washed clean. Blood becomes a permanent stain on the consciences of both characters, and it plagues them throughout life."

STUDY GUIDE

4. DEVELOP AND ORGANIZE ARGUMENTS

The reasons and examples that support your thesis will form the middle paragraphs of your essay. Since you can't really write your thesis statement until you know how you'll structure your argument, you'll probably end up working on steps 3 and 4 at the same time.

There's no single method of argumentation that will work in every context. One essay prompt might ask you to compare and contrast two characters, while another asks you to trace an image through a given work of literature. These questions require different kinds of answers and therefore different kinds of arguments. Below, we'll discuss three common kinds of essay prompts and some strategies for constructing a solid, well-argued case.

TYPES OF LITERARY ESSAYS
Compare and contrast

Compare and contrast the characters of King Lear *and* Gloucester *in* King Lear.

Chances are you've written this kind of essay before. In an academic literary context, you'll organize your arguments the same way you would in any other class. You can either go *subject by subject* or *point by point*. In the former, you'll discuss one character first and then the second. In the latter, you'll choose several traits (attitude toward life, social status, images and metaphors associated with the character) and devote a paragraph to each. You may want to use a mix of these two approaches—for example, you may want to spend a paragraph apiece broadly sketching King Lear's and Gloucester's personalities before transitioning into a paragraph or two describing a few key points of comparison. This can be a highly effective strategy if you want to make a counterintuitive argument—that, despite seeming to be totally different, the two objects being compared are actually similar in a very important way (or vice versa). Remember that your essay should reveal something fresh or unexpected about the text, so think beyond the obvious parallels and differences.

Trace

Choose an image—for example, birds, knives, or eyes—and trace that image throughout Macbeth.

Sounds pretty easy, right? All you need to do is read the play, underline every appearance of a knife in *Macbeth,* and then list them in your essay in the order they appear, right? Well, not exactly. Your teacher doesn't want a simple catalog of examples. He or she wants to see you make *connections* between those examples—that's the difference between summarizing and analyzing. In the *Macbeth* example above, think about the different contexts in which knives appear in the play and to what effect. In *Macbeth,* there are real knives and imagined knives; knives that kill and knives that simply threaten. Categorize and classify your examples to give them some order. Finally, always keep the overall effect in mind. After you choose and analyze your examples, you should come to some greater understanding about the work, as well as your chosen image, symbol, or phrase's role in developing the major themes and stylistic strategies of that work.

Debate

Does Iago in Othello *hate women?*

In this kind of essay, you're being asked to debate a moral, ethical, or aesthetic issue regarding the work. You might be asked to judge a character or group of characters (*Is Caesar responsible for his own demise?*) or the work itself (*Is* Romeo and Juliet *a feminist play?*). For this kind of essay, there are two important points to keep in mind. First, don't simply base your arguments on your personal feelings and reactions. Every literary essay expects you to read and analyze the work, so search for evidence in the text. What does Iago have to say about women in *Othello?* How does Iago treat women in *Othello?* As in any debate, you also need to make sure that you define all the necessary terms before you begin to argue your case.

What does it mean to hate a whole gender? What makes a play feminist? You should define your terms right up front, in the first paragraph after your introduction.

Second, remember that strong literary essays make contrary and surprising arguments. Try to think outside the box. In the *Othello* example above, it seems like the obvious answer would be yes, Iago hates women. But can you think of any arguments for the opposite side? Even if your final assertion is that the play depicts an angry, misogynistic man who distrusts women, acknowledging and responding to the counterargument will strengthen your overall case.

5. WRITE THE INTRODUCTION

Your introduction sets up the entire essay. It's where you present your topic and articulate the particular issues and questions you'll be addressing. It's also where you, as the writer, introduce yourself to your readers. A persuasive literary essay immediately establishes its writer as a knowledgeable, authoritative figure.

An introduction can vary in length depending on the overall length of the essay, but in a traditional five-paragraph essay it should be no longer than one paragraph. However long it is, your introduction needs to:

Provide any necessary context. Your introduction should situate the reader and let him or her know what to expect. What book are you discussing? Which characters? What topic will you be addressing?

Answer the "So what?" question. Why is this topic important, and why is your particular position on the topic noteworthy? Ideally, your introduction should pique the reader's interest by suggesting how your argument is surprising or otherwise counterintuitive. Literary essays make unexpected connections and reveal less-than-obvious truths.

Present your thesis. This usually happens at or very near the end of your introduction.

Indicate the shape of the essay to come. Your reader should finish reading your introduction with a good sense of the scope of your essay as well as the path you'll take toward proving your thesis. You don't need to spell out every step, but you do need to suggest the organizational pattern you'll be using.

Your introduction should not:

Be vague. Beware of the two killer words in literary analysis: *interesting* and *important*. Of course the work, question, or example is interesting and important—that's why you're writing about it!

Open with any grandiose assertions. Many student readers think that beginning their essays with a flamboyant statement such as "Since the dawn of time, writers have been fascinated with the topic of free will" makes them sound important and commanding. You know what? It actually sounds pretty amateurish.

Wildly praise the work. Another typical mistake student writers make is extolling the work or author. Your teacher doesn't need to be told that "Shakespeare is perhaps the greatest writer in the English language." You can mention a work's reputation in passing—by referring to *Romeo and Juliet* as "Shakespeare's enduring classic," for example— but don't make a point of bringing it up unless that reputation is key to your argument.

Go off-topic. Keep your introduction streamlined and to the point. Don't feel the need to throw in all kinds of bells and whistles in order to impress your reader—just get to the point as quickly as you can without skimping on any of the required steps.

6. WRITE THE BODY PARAGRAPHS

Once you've written your introduction, you'll take the arguments you developed in step 4 and turn them into your body paragraphs. The organization of this middle section of your essay will largely be determined by the argumentative strategy you use, but no matter how you arrange your thoughts, your body paragraphs need to do the following:

Begin with a strong topic sentence. Topic sentences are like signs on a highway: they tell the readers where they are and where they're going. A good topic sentence not only alerts readers to what issue will be discussed in the following paragraph but also gives them a sense of what argument will be made about that issue. "Jealousy plays an important role in *A Midsummer Night's Dream*" isn't a strong topic sentence because it doesn't tell us very much. "Jealousy plays out most obviously among the quartet of Athenian lovers, who find themselves in an increasingly tangled knot of misaligned desire" is a much stronger topic sentence—it not only tells us what the paragraph will discuss (jealousy) but how the paragraph will discuss the topic (by showing how jealousy creates a set of conditions that leads to the play's climactic action).

Fully and completely develop a single thought. Don't skip around in your paragraph or try to stuff in too much material. Body paragraphs are like bricks: each individual one needs to be strong and sturdy or else the entire structure will collapse. Make sure you have really proven your point before moving on to the next one.

Use transitions effectively. Good literary essay writers know that each paragraph must be clearly and strongly linked to the material around it. Think of each paragraph as a response to the one that precedes it. Use transition words and phrases such as *however, similarly, on the contrary, therefore,* and *furthermore* to indicate what kind of response you're making.

7. WRITE THE CONCLUSION

Just as you used the introduction to ground your readers in the topic before providing your thesis, you'll use the conclusion to quickly summarize the specifics learned thus far and then hint at the broader implications of your topic. A good conclusion will:

Do more than simply restate the thesis. If your thesis argued that *The Merchant of Venice* can be read as a study of religious differences, don't simply end your essay by saying, "And that is why *The Merchant of Venice* can be read as a study of religious differences." If you've constructed your arguments well, this kind of statement would just be redundant.

Synthesize the arguments, not summarize them. Similarly, don't repeat the details of your body paragraphs in your conclusion. The readers have already read your essay, and chances are it's not so long that they've forgotten all your points by now.

Revisit the "So what?" question. In your introduction, you made a case for why your topic and position were important. You should close your essay with the same sort of gesture. What do your readers know now that they didn't know before? How will that knowledge help them better appreciate or understand the work overall?

Move from the specific to the general. Your essay has most likely treated a very specific element of the work— a single character, a small set of images, or a particular passage. In your conclusion, try to show how this narrow discussion has wider implications for the work overall. If your essay on *The Tempest* focused on the character of Prospero, for example, you might want to include a bit in your conclusion about how he fits into the play's larger message about power, humanity, or the pursuit of knowledge.

Stay relevant. Your conclusion should suggest new directions of thought, but it shouldn't be treated as an opportunity to pad your essay with all the extra, interesting ideas you came up with during your brainstorming sessions but couldn't fit into the essay proper. Don't attempt to stuff in unrelated queries or too many abstract thoughts.

Avoid making overblown closing statements.
A conclusion should open up your highly specific, focused discussion, but it should do so without drawing a sweeping lesson about life or human nature. Making such observations may be part of the point of reading, but it's almost always a mistake in essays, where these observations tend to sound overly dramatic or simply silly.

A+ ESSAY CHECKLIST

Congratulations! If you've followed all the steps we've outlined above, you should have a solid literary essay to show for all your efforts. What if you've got your sights set on an A+? To write the kind of superlative essay that will be rewarded with a perfect grade, keep the following rubric in mind. These are the qualities that teachers expect to see in a truly A+ essay. How does yours stack up?

- Demonstrates a thorough understanding of the book
- Presents an original, compelling argument
- Thoughtfully analyzes the text's formal elements
- Uses appropriate and insightful examples
- Structures ideas in a logical and progressive order
- Demonstrates a mastery of sentence construction, transitions, grammar, spelling, and word choice

SUGGESTED ESSAY TOPICS

1. Discuss the relationship between Antonio and Bassanio. What does their friendship reveal about their characters?

2. Examine Shylock's rhetoric. Pay special attention to the quality of his language—his use of metaphor and repetition, for instance. How do his speeches reflect his character as a whole?

3. Compare and contrast Venice and Belmont. What is the significance of these distinct settings in the play?

4. Analyze the way that time passes in *The Merchant of Venice*, paying special attention to conflicts between time in Venice and Belmont. Are there any inconsistencies, and if so, how does the play handle them?

5. To what extent is Shylock defined by his Jewishness? To what extent is he defined by his profession?

6. Discuss Portia's character. How does she compare to the men around her? Is Bassanio a worthy husband for her?

A+ STUDENT ESSAY

Examine the courtroom scene in The Merchant of Venice.

HOW DOES IT ILLUMINATE THE PLAY'S MAJOR THEMES?

Shakespeare's courtroom scene dramatizes a conflict between justice and mercy—the competing claims of an angry Shylock and a desperate Bassanio. This argument mirrors several smaller disputes and personal crises throughout *The Merchant of Venice*. Shakespeare's characters must frequently weigh their sense of grievance against their sense of generosity. By placing the conflict at the center of his play, Shakespeare suggests that the pains of sacrifice are inescapable. It is human to resent, and it is human to forgive.

The courtroom scene enacts a crisis all humans must someday face: whether to pardon an enemy or insist on revenge. Portia speaks on behalf of mercy, arguing that we must always forgive one another because we are constantly hoping for our own share of forgiveness from an all-knowing God. Likewise, the Duke demonstrates the virtues of mercy when he ignores the letter of the law and waves away his right to take Shylock's life. On the other hand, Shylock represents the all-too-human desire for justice. He has evidence of Antonio's oath and simply wants to carry out the terms of the agreement. Portia frightens him when she begins to argue in Shylock's own terms. Invoking the supremacy of justice, she says he may have a pound of flesh but not a drop of blood, with the threatened penalty of death if he does not follow her terms exactly. Mercy and justice—forgiveness and vengeance—spar relentlessly in this climactic scene.

Shakespeare has laid the thematic groundwork for his climax by repeatedly noting the virtues of a merciful way of life. Antonio takes on heroic stature when he forgives Bassanio's countless debts and encourages him to find love. Portia tempers Nerissa's severity when she says we must be merciful unto others as well as unto ourselves. Portia forgives Bassanio for leaving Belmont on the night of their engagement, putting aside her own wishes and encouraging him to help his friend. Jessica and Lorenzo repeatedly note the necessity of good humor; it is in the nature of lovers to stray and to make false promises, so we must try to laugh and see what is best in one another. Each of these characters acts as an occasional spokes person for the mild-mannered, magnanimous approach to life.

On the other hand, several of Shakespeare's characters crave justice in moments of weakness. Despite his constant sacrifices, Antonio becomes irritating when he seems to brood on his sense of perpetual martyrdom, and Gratiano urges him to abandon his silent grievances and enjoy his life. Long before the courtroom scene, Shylock embodies the human desire for revenge, asking why he should cooperate with Antonio when Antonio has ignored him and called him a cur. The Prince of Arragon seems absurd when he claims Portia on the grounds that he deserves her, and the message in the silver casket rebukes him for thinking that we are ever naturally entitled to happiness. In our discomfort and self-absorption, we make the error of Shakespeare's characters and insist on justice in a patently unjust world.

By pitting mercy against justice in his climactic scene, Shakespeare suggests that everyone struggles with competing urges to complain and forgive. Shylock demands the flesh the law has promised him, and Portia argues that the world is too complex to be governed by rigid laws. Portia, Antonio, and Lorenzo all occasionally look past their own problems and behave generously, whereas other characters cannot overcome a gnawing sense of grievance and injustice. In five tolerant, effortless acts, Shakespeare shows us that we are destined to have these arguments—with others and with ourselves—every day of our lives.

GLOSSARY OF LITERARY TERMS

Antagonist
The entity that acts to frustrate the goals of the protagonist. The antagonist is usually another character but may also be a non-human force.

Antihero / Antiheroine
A protagonist who is not admirable or who challenges notions of what should be considered admirable.

Character
A person, animal, or any other thing with a personality that appears in a narrative.

Climax
The moment of greatest intensity in a text or the major turning point in the plot.

Conflict
The central struggle that moves the plot forward. The conflict can be the protagonist's struggle against fate, nature, society, or another person.

First-person point of view
A literary style in which the narrator tells the story from his or her own point of view and refers to himself or herself as "I." The narrator may be an active participant in the story or just an observer.

Hero / Heroine
The principal character in a literary work or narrative.

Imagery
Language that brings to mind sense-impressions, representing things that can be seen, smelled, heard, tasted, or touched.

Motif
A recurring idea, structure, contrast, or device that develops or informs the major themes of a work of literature.

Narrative
A story.

Narrator
The person (sometimes a character) who tells a story; the voice assumed by the writer. The narrator and the author of the work of literature are not necessarily the same person.

Plot
The arrangement of the events in a story, including the sequence in which they are told, the relative emphasis they are given, and the causal connections between events.

Point of View
The perspective that a narrative takes toward the events it describes.

Protagonist
The main character around whom the story revolves.

Setting
The location of a narrative in time and space. Setting creates mood or atmosphere.

Subplot
A secondary plot that is of less importance to the overall story but that may serve as a point of contrast or comparison to the main plot.

Symbol
An object, character, figure, or color that is used to represent an abstract idea or concept. Unlike an emblem, a symbol may have different meanings in different contexts.

Syntax
The way the words in a piece of writing are put together to form lines, phrases, or clauses; the basic structure of a piece of writing.

Theme
A fundamental and universal idea explored in a literary work.

STUDY GUIDE

Tone
The author's attitude toward the subject or characters of a story or poem or toward the reader.

Voice
An author's individual way of using language to reflect his or her own personality and attitudes. An author communicates voice through tone, diction, and syntax.

A NOTE ON PLAGIARISM

Plagiarism—presenting someone else's work as your own—rears its ugly head in many forms. Many students know that copying text without citing it is unacceptable. But some don't realize that even if you're not quoting directly, but instead are paraphrasing or summarizing, it is plagiarism unless you cite the source.

HERE ARE THE MOST COMMON FORMS OF PLAGIARISM:

- Using an author's phrases, sentences, or paragraphs without citing the source

- Paraphrasing an author's ideas without citing the source

- Passing off another student's work as your own

HOW DO YOU STEER CLEAR OF PLAGIARISM?

- You should always acknowledge all words and ideas that aren't your own by using quotation marks around verbatim text or citations like footnotes and end-notes to note another writer's ideas.

- For more information on how to give credit when credit is due, ask your teacher for guidance or visit www.sparknotes.com.